BUILDING FROM BELIEF

Advance, Retreat, and Compromise in the Remaking of Catholic Church Architecture

Michael E. DeSanctis

THE LITURGICAL PRESS
Collegeville, Minnesota

www.litpress.org

Design by David Manahan, O.S.B. Cover photograph: St. John the Baptist Church, interior detail, Erie, Pennsylvania. Photo by Michael E. DeSanctis.

2   3   4   5   6   7   8   9

ISBN 0-8146-2755-2

For Laura

CONTENTS

ACKNOWLEDGMENTS

The essays included in this book have previously appeared in the pages of *Emmanuel* magazine, *Liturgy 90,* and *E&A: Environment and Art Letter.* I wish to thank the publishers for kindly extending me permission to reprint my words and images here. Particular thanks go to Rev. Eugene LaVerdiere, s.s.s., and Rev. Anthony Schueller, s.s.s., editors of *Emmanuel,* whose invitation in 1995 to produce a series of articles on Catholic church architecture for that publication's centenary became the germ of *Building from Belief.* I must also acknowledge the assistance of David Philippart of Liturgy Training Publications, whose frequent collaborations over the years have proven very rewarding. I am indebted to David for his sound editorial judgment, and for reminding me through frequent phone calls from Chicago that there exists a vital and complex community of American Catholics beyond the boundaries of the country's northeastern dioceses.

I would be remiss if I did not mention here the consistent support and friendship of Msgr. Conrad L. Kraus, director of the Office of Worship in the Diocese of Erie, Pennsylvania. Msgr. Kraus entered the priesthood many years ago in order to serve the People of God. Anyone who has observed Conrad in his service to the liturgical life of the Church cannot help but be struck by the selflessness with which he continues to conduct his ministry, even today. Msgr. Kraus was gracious enough to review the contents of this book in their preliminary forms, and his insights and criticism are greatly appreciated.

This work is dedicated to my wife, Laura, for the simple reason that it could never have been produced without her cooperation. Laura has freed me to ruminate on the fine points of church architecture by attending daily (hourly!) to the four children who now surround us in a church pew each Sunday morning, who sustain our faith and make our lives blessed ones. I dedicate this work to my wife with deepest affection, and with confidence that the Church she is helping so tangibly to build up will be freely embraced by yet another generation of Christ's followers.

PREFACE

As a bishop, one of the most enjoyable and prayerful liturgies for which I preside is the dedication of a church. Parishioners are proud of their achievements, liturgies are planned with special attention, pastors are often humbled by what has been accomplished through their simple gifts, and on the day when the focus is on the building, it is never more evident to me that the Church is the People of God.

Sometimes these buildings are new creations; sometimes a reordering of an existing structure; always they are an experience of grace working through bricks and glass, through committees and inspiration, and through the Word made flesh dwelling among us.

Dr. Michael DeSanctis has written an explosive little book—explosive in terms of the number of ideas incorporated into every page and every sentence. A natural-born teacher, he lines up a number of topics that have to do with the creation and use of liturgical space and then clearly treats each one in detail. Knowledge of the historical development of both the Church and its architecture is evident. The footnotes are a veritable library of the field.

If there is one thesis that holds this volume together, it is the need for teaching—for catechesis. And a necessary component of catechesis is "conversion." Dr. DeSanctis dreams of a change of heart on the part of the worshiping community, of the building committee, of the professionals involved in the design process, and, yes, of the Church at large. Thus, this volume is about hope and courage.

I am particularly impressed with the author's ease with the theological concepts of grace and sacramentality. He offers rich insights to these fundamental Christian realities to the reader as graciously as God does to his people. There is an undeniable excitement in his writing about using the gifts that we have been given.

I am impressed as well with the chapter in which pastors express their feelings about the building or renovation process. Other pastors will want to learn from them. The dying and rising of the Lord Jesus is evident in their stories. Since there may not be a seminary course in this area, this book could be most helpful.

Dr. DeSanctis invites members of parishes to a ministry that is not usually listed in indices of liturgical and pastoral ministry texts. He invites those who are involved in the creation of worship space to be "the world's memory of what beauty looks like, what sanctity feels like" (chapter 1). Readers and parish committees can only be inspired and comforted to know that they can be the instruments of truth and beauty. (Can you imagine what town-hall meetings *could* be like?)

In thanking Dr. DeSanctis for sharing his faith, his passion about art and beauty, his insights into the working of the Divine in what looks like a messy human situation, and his splendid gift of teaching—I look forward to my next invitation to celebrate the *Dedication of a Church and Altar.*

Most Reverend Donald W. Trautman, STD, SSL
Bishop of Erie

INTRODUCTION:
"WHERE WE STAND"

It is said that when Lewis Mumford offered his pioneering courses in urban planning at universities across the United States he took particular pleasure in leading students through actual city streets—through alleyways, in fact, and fish markets, playgrounds, parks, waterfronts, and slum tenements. Mumford was not one to treat the city as an abstraction, nor was he satisfied with academic explanations of how urban environments were supposed to behave. Instead he impressed upon his students the importance of observing firsthand how real people, living in real conditions, are affected by the physical structures that surround them. In the immediate, visceral data of the streets lay the clues to why cities succeeded or failed, Mumford believed, and it was the proper business of persons wanting to improve city life by means of design to regard such clues with care.

It is in the spirit of Mumford's work that I offer the observations compiled in this book, having recognized long ago the inconsistency that often exists between the way the Roman Catholic Church speaks of its liturgical arts in legislative and scholarly statements and the manner in which it actually practices them. As much as I have intended to explain the important theoretical foundations of recent Catholic church design in light of the liturgical reforms of the Second Vatican Council, my greater goal has been to assess the state of sacred architecture as one finds it operating today in average, American parish communities. Indeed, much of what I offer here is inspired by my work as a design consultant to parishes involved in the construction of new places of worship or the reconfiguration of existing ones. I have also drawn from personal experiences of the liturgical settings maintained by parochial communities to which I myself have belonged, where, in the company of loved ones and friends, I have been able to consider with greatest emotional involvement the ways in which architecture asserts itself on the regular celebrations of the local church—containing them, shaping them, and generally adding to the rich complement of sight and sound that is rightly described as "sacramental."

In the course of helping parishes address the challenges of liturgical design unique to our time, I have been welcomed by American Catholics of every stripe into the places where they allow themselves to be most candid, most vulnerable, most open to the confusion and doubt that together accompany institutional change. Their accounts of how the reform of sacred architecture has played out at the local level should give pause to anyone who underestimates the complexity of the matter or believes too easily in what has been called "the doctrine of salvation by bricks."[1] Though it is fashionable for those in liturgical arts circles to outline in simple, cause-and-effect terms how changes in the spatial accommodations for Catholic liturgy will inevitably precipitate changes in the way the faithful themselves behave when assembled for worship, my experience suggests that no easily predictable relationship exists between design and use in buildings for an ecclesial body as diverse in its membership as ours. Architecture affects human behavior, to be sure. But it does so subtly, subliminally—by suggestion not coercion—and, like any mode of artistic expression, it is always susceptible to misinterpretation or total disregard by those not disposed to receiving its message.

In one parish whose church building I recently helped to remodel, for example, certain worshipers are so intent upon viewing the tabernacle during liturgical services that they situate themselves in a newly constructed eucharistic reservation chapel, separated by a wall of glass from other members of the assembly, to the puzzlement of the pastor, the building committee, and the architect who planned the space. At another community I know of, whose intimate arrangement of liturgical furnishings was intended expressly to unify worshipers, large numbers of parishioners choose to stand at the entrance doors during services, disengaging themselves from the actions unfolding round them. And in yet other locale, where a comprehensive reordering of the liturgical environment was supposed to have deepened parishioners' reverence for the sacred, it has become common for choir members to collate sheet music on the elegant, counter-like parapet installed to distance the tabernacle

1. This adage is attributed to the theologian Reinhold Niebuhr. See Jane Jacobs, *The Life and Death of Great American Cities* (New York: Vantage, 1961) 113.

from the altar of sacrifice, an act that trivializes the new appointment, to say nothing of the sacramental presence of Christ enshrined nearby.

Such scenarios clearly point to the ongoing need for adult catechesis in our parishes—a theme to which I frequently return in the following pages. Yet, even in communities whose liturgical and aesthetic formation is judged to be fairly advanced, there can be a marked difference between the intended effect of the place prepared for worship and the patterns of popular use that emerge spontaneously within it. The Church's current architectural practice is guided by the loftiest of ideals. It presupposes a degree of willingness on the part of the Catholic faithful to accept the gentle, corrective nudging of enveloping wall planes, floors, and ceilings designed to revise their habits of corporate prayer. But in the workaday reality of the parish, there is often little appreciation for liturgical-architectural idealism and a tendency to treat the weaknesses inherent in a familiar place of worship with casual indifference. This is clearly the case in one parish with which I am familiar that literally outgrew its church building years ago. So cramped are conditions for weekend liturgies in the nave of the parish's exceedingly narrow, basilican-style structure that many worshipers are relegated to side aisles, where they must sit on rickety folding chairs in the shadows of massive, load-bearing piers. Others—the perennial "overflow"—occupy an abandoned choir loft at the rear of the liturgical space, requiring them virtually to reenact the Exodus migration story each time they wish to join in a Communion procession. There is little that is inspiring about the general appearance of this place, as time and misuse have robbed it of its original beauty. The lighting is poor, the furnishings of the sanctuary are second-rate, and the restroom facilities, located in a dark and dangerous basement, are inaccessible to all but the most able-bodied of worshipers. Parishioners readily admit that their building is less than adequate but as yet have found neither the will nor the resources to make necessary improvements. Like homeowners who have grown blind to leaky faucets, broken doorknobs or threadbare carpets, they are able to disregard the deficiencies in their house of prayer, which they see as diminishing little from the autonomous beauty of divine worship itself. These are issues that most members of the community confront only once a week, after all, during visits to a building that last for barely an hour. The Mass and its setting are somehow exempted from the rules of analysis and qualitative judgment and treated like passing experiences, with as much staying power as the contents of the weekly bulletin.

When American Catholics of average means *are* pressed to reflect more than superficially on the state of sacred architecture, they concede to being only mildly satisfied with the new or modified places that serve them on occasions of public worship but uncertain of what it is precisely that leaves them wanting. At the public forums that are now regular parts of the typical parish building project, one hears the voices of persons still bewildered by changes in the norms for communal prayer and, as much, perhaps, by their own diminished interest in discussing the subject. "I'm tired of fighting about the Mass and what liturgists say is the right way to build a church," a middle-age laywoman confessed aloud at a recent parish-wide discussion I moderated, even as her community prepared to celebrate completion of a long and controversial building campaign. "After thirty-five years of trying to keep up with all these changes in the way we pray, I just don't care anymore—and I'm not even sure I'm going to enjoy worshiping in our new building."

Sentiments like these are not uncommon, for the superheated atmosphere of liturgical renewal that succeeded Vatican II seems to have cooled considerably. Gone is the riotous, experimental mood that seized parishes in the 1960s and 1970s, which, while no doubt fostering some mistreatment of the Church's patrimony of art and architecture, nevertheless gave evidence of a religious body pulsing with life. In its wake a certain weariness has beset priests and laypeople alike, leaving them less inclined to debate the course liturgical design should assume at the outset of a new millennium than simply to accept the ambivalence that pervades this aspect of contemporary Catholic life.

What one does *not* detect in American parishes, I hasten to note, is an overwhelming desire on the part of the faithful merely to return to the canons of design predating Vatican II, when church buildings, however large or impressive, were anything but "user-friendly." Catholics in the United States have grown too attached to the comfort and convenience built into every other corner of the public domain to tolerate religious spaces that do not attend to their practical, human needs. A new church building without proper restrooms or nursery facilities, for example, is unimaginable today, as is one in which worshipers, packed into pews, must shiver during the winter months, sweat in the summer, or routinely suffer the effects of bad acoustics. Certainly every parish has its contingent of self-described "traditionalists," who believe there is something edifying about the minor discomforts one experiences in buildings erected prior to the reforms of recent decades. ("Years ago we went to church to pray, and the focus was on God," says one laywoman, "not on whether we were comfortable, or whether there were changing tables for our babies, or places for us to hang up our coats.") These are often the most vocal critics of clerical leaders, quick to dismantle the reputation of a reform-minded priest or bishop in order to preserve intact the fabric of some cherished edifice, and the loudness of their protest may suggest that their views hold sway with Catholics at large.

What most Mass-goers want in their places of worship, however, is not something older or more exotic but simply something *better* than that to which they have been introduced in recent decades. When one hears the lament, "Why can't we build churches the way we did in the old days?" it should be taken more as a judgment on the quality of materials and crafts- manship associated with older buildings than on the appropriateness of their designs to the needs of modern American Catholic piety. Frankly, the mean- ing behind many of the fixtures of pre-Vatican II architecture is lost on Ameri- can Catholics today, whose knowledge of the Church's own artistic and iconographic heritage is limited.[2] Church buildings cast in contemporary styles fare no better, oddly enough, because they require their users to extract meaning from the sparest, most understated of forms. It has been my experi- ence that the artful play of simplified exterior geometry common to these structures goes largely unnoticed, compromised as it is by the vast, asphalt planes of the parking lots that surround them, and their austere interiors are almost universally dismissed as "cold," "bland," and "impersonal." For those believers who long for nothing more than the sheer solidity of Catholic build- ings constructed before Vatican II, the admittedly flimsy appearance of many newer structures is emblematic of all that recently has gone wrong with the Church and of the tenuousness of Catholic culture in general. It is, under- standably, a frightening time for those who measure the substance of the Church's teachings by the literal substantiality of the buildings it erects.

Circumstances beyond the control of local faith communities have a sig- nificant influence on the quality of sacred architecture today, however, not the least of which are the restrictive economic conditions under which they must function when committing to a large-scale architectural venture. Prospective contributors to capital fund drives are regularly surprised to learn how little an initial resource of, say, two million dollars will procure their parish in the course of erecting a new worship facility—even more surprised when they dis- cover how costly an undertaking the renovation of a standing edifice can be.

---

2. On this score I remain steadfastly in disagreement with such observers of American Catholicism as Rev. Andrew Greeley, who routinely give the faithful high marks for cultural-artistic literacy. Building upon the work of Rev. David Tracy, Father Greeley has for years been arguing that the "analogical imagination" possessed by American Catholics makes them more inclined to understand and appreciate sacramental- artistic expression than their Protestant counterparts. (See, for example, "Catholics, Fine Arts and the Li- turgical Imagination," *America* [May 18, 1996] 9–14.) My experience with parish communities across the country suggests rather that Catholics know remarkably little about the history, rites or artistic traditions of their church and are often the products of diocesan schools, colleges, and universities that placed little emphasis on arts education.

The charitable giving habits of Catholic laypeople themselves have changed, making it difficult for some parishes to amass even a portion of the funds necessary to build and furnish a place of worship appropriately. Whereas previous generations of immigrant Catholics in the United States gave freely of their limited resources to erect monuments of religious and ethnic pride, the members of today's thoroughly naturalized church, though wealthier than their predecessors, give reluctantly, with demands for assurances that their monetary contributions be spent only in ways that they see fit. I have heard Catholics in their seventies and eighties, who helped finance development of the Church's expansive, post-World War II, suburban complexes, argue that they should be exempted from having to support building projects again, at the close of their lives. "My wife and I helped build the church, rectory, and convent in this parish," one retired layman explained to me. "We built the school and paid to send all our kids there. If we have to update everything in our church to conform to Vatican II, let the younger parishioners pay for it! It's their turn now!" Conversely, young, upwardly mobile Catholic professionals like to complain that it is not yet time for them to shoulder the burden of maintaining the Church's architectural monuments, which are occupied throughout the workweek mostly by the elderly and retired. In parishes where either kind of thinking prevails, architectural projects can face serious underfunding, which usually means that aesthetic and expressive values are subordinated to some vaguely defined paradigm of "functionality."

The way in which architecture is increasingly practiced in the United States likewise affects the quality of what Catholics observe in their places of worship. Small, detail-oriented firms, given to slow and methodical refinement of design ideas, are the exception today. More common are the large but mercilessly efficient "production shops," which, in order to operate within relatively modest profit margins, must concern themselves more with the *volume* of building projects they turn out annually than with the degree to which their works achieve the status of high art. Describing the architectural enterprise as a long and patient distillation process yielding buildings of exceptional beauty invites grins and embarrassed laughter from practitioners themselves, who are quick to note that even ecclesiastical clients today are more interested in "fast-tracking" their way to some passable solution to an architectural problem than in committing themselves to the protracted, trial-and-error process required of artistic greatness. "Clients like to see something tangible for their money," one architect explains, "and they don't like spending a lot of dollars in the early stages of a project to have me explore all the design possibilities their needs suggest." "Most church groups have to be 'backed into' a building anyway," adds another architect, implying that the plans for many attractive and liturgically sound buildings must be scaled down or diluted artistically to accommodate parishes' conservative project budgets.

In an effort to maintain the business of today's exceedingly cost-conscious clients, architects in some markets are willing to establish so-called "design-build" partnerships with construction firms, a practice that has emerged in recent years as a major industry trend.[3] Arrangements like these, which temporarily consolidate the respective providers of design and construction services, are attractive to church groups, as they can shorten considerably the time required to conceive, design, and erect a place of worship. They can also help reduce the redundant costs associated with documentation and inter-office communication parishes incur when retaining the separate services of architects, engineers, specialized consultants, and other professional participants in the building process. For pastors and parish committees daunted by the sheer logistical complexity of an architectural project, conducting business with a single, corporate entity can simply seem easier, from a strictly psychological perspective, than dealing with several. "The whole process is streamlined," one parish administrator remarks enthusiastically, "so I only have to cut one check at the end of the month."

If there is a danger that design-build schemes pose to parishes with architectural aspirations, however, it is simply that they can compromise the participating architects' ability to act in the best interest of their clients should questions arise about the artistic or symbolic integrity of proposed church buildings. Traditionally, architects have been able to serve as advocates for their clients and defenders of good design by standing apart from those parties responsible for the actual fabrication of buildings. Their broad purview over the architectural process has thus included responsibility for determining a client's needs, for translating those needs into necessary technical drawings, and for ensuring by personal supervision that the edifice which results is, in the profession's time-honored dictum, "useable, well-built, and beautiful." What happens too often today, when responsibility for the creation of a building is shared among the various participants in a design-build collaborative, is

3. Industry observers suggest that over 80 percent of major construction projects in the United States now conform to design-build procedures. In the seven-year period between 1986 and 1993, design-build projects increased from approximately $25 billion of new contract volume among the country's 400 top contractors to $71 billion—a third of the group's new contract volume. See Sandra San Agustin, "Design-Build Is Becoming an Industry Trend," *Source News and Reports*, 16 October 1995. http:sddt.com/files/library/95headlines/DN95_10_16/STORY95_10_16_08.html. Two useful explanations of the practical and legal implications of the design-build method are found respectively in Carl F. Wesely, "Design-Build: Why It's the Hottest Trend in Contracting," *Design-Build* (July 1997) 16, and Gordon Hunt, "An Attorney Looks at Design-Build: Wave of the Future?" *Design-Build* (March 1996) 24–26.

that the architect is reduced to little more than a drafter or renderer, dutifully producing images of buildings on paper but with limited control over their appearance when constructed. One of the most common abuses of design-build partnerships in fact occurs when design-altering decisions about a building are made for purely budgetary reasons by someone *other than* the architect, who is retained largely to meet the requirements of certain state or municipal codes. What is sacrificed first in buildings "value-engineered" into being by a team of construction management specialists are the very qualities that have always distinguished greater architecture from lesser, sacred structures from the basely utilitarian: the essential poetry of the place, the care with which its finish materials have been handled, and the degree to which its form conveys a sense of unity, resolution, and completeness. If it is true, as the great, modernist architect Mies van der Rohe liked to assert, that God resides "in the details,"[4] then it may well be the spark of divinity that is missing from many of the church buildings American Catholics currently behold, or at least the divinely inspired supervision of a competent architect.

Even in those contemporary Catholic church-building projects that result from a more immediate relationship between architect and edifice, the ability of the former to steer the work at hand in the direction of highest artistic quality can be frustrated by what I perceive to be a multiplication of agendas, or what might be called the "too many cooks" syndrome. To understand this point, one must remember that prior to Vatican II the procedures for erecting a parish church building in the United States were relatively straightforward and involved few participants. The planning and preliminary design discussions, such as they were, took place in rectory dining rooms and studies, far removed from the scrutiny of anyone but the pastor, a favored architect, and perhaps the resident clergy. Drawings for a place of worship, based upon centuries of canonically prescribed models, could be developed by an architect in timely fashion with little confusion of purpose and with a nod to the particular tastes of the pastor-patron and the local bishop. The process worked well; it was fluid, succinct, and left no doubt in the architect's mind whose intentions were to serve as the starting point of the design process. If the lay members of the parish had any part in the enterprise at all, it was simply to retire the debt on the completed building as quickly as possible when called upon to do so. Church-planning was essentially a cultic, clerical activity, like the "Secret" of the old Tridentine Rite Mass, but involving hushed intonations over coffee tables and drafting tables as opposed to the surface of some holy mensa.

4. Among other places, Mies's famous axiom is recorded in Peter Blake, *Mies van der Rohe: Architecture and Structure* (New York: Penguin, 1960) 62.

In contrast, so inclusive are the means parishes employ when planning their liturgical accommodations today that architects can find themselves hard-pressed to determine from whom they should take their cues. There is first, in every church-building project, the implicit guidance of "the documents," those official, legislative statements on sacred art and architecture promulgated by ecclesiastical agencies at the international, territorial, and diocesan levels. No Catholic building project in the United States is likely to proceed today, for example, without its overseers referring to *Built of Living Stones*, the instruction published in 2000 by the National Conference of Catholic Bishops to replace its earlier *Environment and Art in Catholic Worship*.[5] The passages pertaining to the sacred arts contained in the Constitution on the Sacred Liturgy (*Sacrosanctum concilium*, 1963) of Vatican II and the *General Instruction on the Roman Missal* (1969) are also required reading for those responsible for the construction or renovation of liturgical spaces. Unfortunately, inconsistencies between the contents of these texts and their susceptibility to differences of interpretation render them somewhat less than authoritative. Indeed, it is not uncommon in the context of parish-wide discussion sessions for members of the community opposed to recent liturgical reforms to critique openly the articles of legislation handed down since Vatican II rather than to suggest how they might be applied locally. There is likewise no assurance that all the persons involved in planning deliberations have studied these guidelines in an informed and systematic manner. This is never more apparent than when a pastor and members of a lay building committee arrange a meeting with chancery personnel for the purpose of reviewing the progress of their work. Assembled for these sessions, along with parishioners, their architect and their ordinary, may be a board of episcopal consultors, the director of the local office of worship, representatives of the diocesan commission on art and architecture, and the diocesan facilities manager. Architects hoping to take from such scenes some definitive notion of what is essential to the contemporary liturgical environment are apt to be disappointed. What they discover, more often than not, is that opinions concerning the spatial requirements of Catholic worship vary widely within the Church, and that even those ministers designated the chief liturgists of their dioceses—namely bishops and their immediate, administrative subordinates—are not always as current in their knowledge of liturgical theology, practice and law as they might be. Unaware of the internal politics of a diocesan church, architects may also

---

5. Though welcomed by many church designers at the time of its publication in 1978, *Environment and Art in Catholic Worship* came to be viewed as controversial. Critics of the document asserted that its contents had never been ratified by the entire body of the American Episcopate and that it stressed too greatly the role of the assembly in dictating the sanctity of liturgical buildings (see nos. 28–29).

be caught off guard by the animated squabbling between conferees that can arise at the discussion table.

At one meeting of this kind I recall, considerable time was spent by those present simply working out a common language to facilitate discussion. One participant, a cathedral rector, was surprised to learn that the word "bema" was part of modern Catholic parlance and not exclusively "a Jewish term." Another thought it inappropriate to speak of the presence of "vestries" in Catholic church buildings, a word that, in his opinion, "we stole from the Episcopalians." A third dismissed altogether the phrase "worship space," thinking it part of a pernicious campaign by liberals in the Church to Protestantize the nomenclature of Catholic architecture and strip it of its associations with the sacral, the sacerdotal. "Why can't we just call the damned thing a 'church'?" he asked bluntly.

On another occasion I remember, the object of contention was the proposed location of the Blessed Sacrament chapel in a new church building.[6] The architect, thinking he had followed the letter of official legislation by situating the chapel apart from the primary liturgical setting, was surprised to hear the bishop ask aloud, "Shouldn't the priest be able to get to the tabernacle easily during the Mass, in case he runs out of hosts at Communion time?" When the director of the worship office reminded his bishop that, strictly speaking, there was no need for the presider to visit the tabernacle in the course of the Eucharist and, with proper planning, no reason for him to "run out of hosts" during the Communion Rite either, an argument ensued over the general trend in liturgical design toward distinguishing the respective foci of active and passive prayer. A related debate at the chancery of another diocese had the bishop explaining to all present: "The people want to be able to see the tabernacle during Mass. So let's leave it near the altar and not rile them up." The remarks left the attendant architect wondering how to square what he had just heard with the entirely contradictory instructions he had received from the local liturgy director, the latter of whom could only shake his head, dumbfounded.

In the parish social halls and meeting rooms where the bulk of architectural planning is actually accomplished, the impulse toward inclusivity in the church-designing process most often manifests itself in lay committees that

6. The placement of the tabernacle has become perhaps the single most polemical aspect of the typical church-building or renovation project. Those parishioners who conceive of a Catholic church building essentially as a monumental shrine or housing for the Blessed Sacrament quite naturally want to give the tabernacle a place of prominence, from where it may be easily viewed during liturgical services. Those who, contrarily, believe that the purpose of the liturgical environment is essentially to enshrine the living, worshiping, *ecclesial* presence of Christ in the baptized assembly see little need to emphasize the place of Christ's sacramental abidance.

are simply too large and unruly to be effective. During their initial meetings with such groups, architects and related design professionals are again likely to be surprised not only by the diversity of opinions on sacred worship that coexist in the Church but also by the irregularity with which the norms are enforced at the diocesan level. They are apt to be struck, too, by the lack of deference shown their own professional expertise, a reflection of the prevailing attitude in this country that all critical and interpretive opinions carry equal weight. In a culture enthralled with the spectacle and overt egalitarianism of talk radio, talk television, and other, increasingly participatory forums of electronic self-expression, even those design professionals able to command sizable fees for their services are not accorded the kind of popular respect they may have enjoyed in a previous era. A well-established, Pittsburgh-based architectural firm, for instance, was disturbed to discover recently that designs it had developed for one parish's renovation project were being secretly modified by a member of the facilities committee with the help of computer-aided drafting technology. When partners from the firm arrived one evening for a routine meeting with the committee, they were confronted with several mechanically generated variations of their original drawings and an attitude suggesting that their involvement in the project was no longer necessary. The firm promptly ended its association with the parish, convinced that nothing it might offer these clients in the way of professional wisdom could move them beyond their tragically misplaced air of self-sufficiency.

Architects are fond of describing their art as one that is collaborative and participatory; and so it is. Great buildings are not usually produced by an architect working in seclusion. They are born instead of a dialogical process that invites free involvement on the part of both the client and the designer. For this creative dialogue to be productive, it may sometimes require direction, clarification, and definition—tasks that architects willingly assume as part of their important supervisory function. What often happens in the parish setting, however, is that architects are required to adopt a quasi-pastoral role that, far from gaining them a group of more attentive collaborators, makes them the objects of rumor and derision. Vilifying architects is a special habit of Catholic communities, who perceive them as agents of a dramatic sort of change that is likely to be emotionally painful as well as costly. This is especially true in parishes with pastors who have not made liturgical reform a priority or who are weak, tentative, or ineffectual leaders. It is one thing for a familiar parish priest occasionally to mention to his congregation the importance of worshiping as a unified, communal body, quite another thing for someone perceived as both an intruder and a mercenary to enter into the life of a parish with the intention of disrupting the very setting of its most important celebrations.

The horror stories architects trade among themselves about serving Catholic clients are enough to lead some firms consciously to decline commissions for Catholic church work. (One can only guess at the number of gifted artists and architects whose talents have been lost to the Church because of the negative perception that surrounds its treatment of them.) While architects who are themselves Catholic may, out of some natural sense of duty, welcome the opportunity to contribute to the Church's ongoing work of liturgical-artistic renewal, those who are not resent the essentially catechetical responsibilities thrust upon them by an institution that has not seen fit to educate its own members. As one architect, a Presbyterian, admits, "Some of us are reluctant to accept Catholic church jobs, not because the meetings are always at night or because payment is slow in coming, but because we end up having to teach the people things they should already know about their own artistic tradition." What architects "end up having to teach" Catholics is more than just the fundamentals of ecclesiastical art history. There comes a time in most Catholic church-building projects, in fact, when architects begin to realize how ill-equipped their clients are to discuss the theological dimension of liturgy in their parish and its connection to the beliefs of the Church universal. Wanting only to give spatial expression to the common aspirations of a parish, architects must invariably begin to instruct their clients on the fine points of Catholic sacramentality, worship, art, and culture. Often this means inserting a vocabulary into the mouths of parishioners that is not naturally forthcoming. The logic behind this holds that the better a community can articulate its faith, the more meaningfully it will be able to contribute to the planning of an edifice that serves that faith. Architects admit that clients of all kinds must ultimately "design" their own buildings, based upon a well-developed program of practical and aesthetic goals. The special challenge for the religious client, moreover, is to design and build from belief; the sacred structures it erects must rest upon *creedal* foundations that are as deep and true and seamless as any masonry footing formed by human hands. Both foundations are of concern to architects, though it is admittedly easier from their perspective to dictate the conditions of the latter than of the former.

One may gain from all this some greater insight into why there occurs in parishes that build or renovate a curious mimicking of roles between the pastor and the architect. The pastor, though functioning officially as a community's primary liturgist, must gain at least a modicum of fluency in the language and practice of architecture so as to exhort his parishioners to build well and nobly. The architect, though retained primarily for his or her creative abilities, must gain at least a working knowledge of the language and practice of Catholic Christianity so as to inspire clients to worship in a manner consistent with their own religious tradition. The training of seminary and architectural school respectively has not prepared these leaders for their expanded roles, however, which partly explains why there is often a clumsy, seat-of-the-pants quality to the way Catholic church-building projects proceed today. Put simply, the protagonists of contemporary Catholic architecture in this country are really novices at attending to the broader theological, pedagogical, and sociological implications of their work—something the laity have not been slow to detect. "It's like the blind leading the blind," one Catholic professional complains. "Neither the average priest nor the average architect has had a chance to really study liturgy in depth, so they fumble around for a while with committees and meetings and documents, and come up with ideas about church design that are, at best, mediocre and confusing. No wonder nobody's happy."

Masking their insecurity by means of defensiveness or aggression merely compounds the problem for pastors and architects, and, in the opinion of Charles Wilson, writer/editor for the conservative *Christifidelis* newsletter, it is the loyal but cautious parishioner who ultimately feels most abused:

> Virtually all [church] renovation projects are grounded in what the parishioners are told are the needs of the reformed Vatican II liturgy. In fact, they are often motivated by erroneous interpretations of liturgical law. . . . In addition to the physical renovations themselves, the methods by which they are inflicted are of equal or even greater concern. The "process" leading to the actual arrival of bulldozers begins with the appearance of the ubiquitous "experts" and "professionals" who tell the people only what they are supposed to hear. . . . Usually, a renovation committee consisting of carefully selected parishioners emerges to announce the final plans, while any alternative suggestions or proposals are stifled by whatever methods—gentle or not so gentle—that circumstances require. . . . The ever-present "professionals" and "expert consultants" . . . "soften-up" the parishioners with unctuous assurances that "no decisions will be made without everyone having their say." Then . . . all those who have opinions contrary to the outcome desired by the chancery are marginalized or excluded from the discussions by whatever means necessary.[7]

Wilson makes no attempt to hide his disdain for those whom he feels are wrongly destroying the Church's artistic heritage. It is the avowed aim of his publication (as expressed in its masthead) to "defend Catholic truth and uphold Catholic rights." In the context of the above commentary, it is the perceived "liturgical establishment" from whom Wilson and his like-minded

7. Charles Wilson, "ZAP! Your church is renovated! SLAM! Your parish is closed," *Christefidelis* (November 1, 1995) 7.

readers believe the Church needs defending, for it is they who are seeing to it that "communion rails are destroyed, altars are thrust forward like theaters-in-the-round, statues are removed [from buildings] and the Blessed Sacrament [is] banished. . . ."[8] Among those who comprise Wilson's enemy "establishment" are the so-called "liturgical design consultants" who have gained relatively recent admittance to the circle of persons responsible for the planning and designing of Catholic church buildings. So great have the ranks of these professionals grown in the United States that they now enjoy recognition by the American Institute of Architects and such Church-affiliated organizations as the Federation of Diocesan Liturgical Commissions.[9] Indeed, while its roots lie in voluntary ministry to the Church, liturgical design consulting has burgeoned into something of a profitable career field, warranting the formation of a least one national association of practitioners and several certificate-granting institutes designed to train new ones. The guidelines for art and architecture in many American dioceses acknowledge the important contributions design consultants can make to the work of the Church and encourage parishes to seek their assistance at the outset of building and renovation projects.[10] Though the services offered by individual consultants vary widely, in general their presence on a professional design team engaged by a parish is intended to compensate for the inadequacies of expertise in sacred art suffered by pastors, lay committees, and architects. As a student of liturgical theory, history, and design, it is the consultant who guides the work of parishes in ways consistent with the Church's stated norms for modern worship.

Perhaps it is their novelty in the realm of Catholic architecture or the inherently prophetic nature of the work they do that makes liturgical design consultants a favorite target of opponents of liturgical reform. Often the attacks are *ad hominem*, as they were in a recent issue of the publication *Catholic Dossier*[11] devoted entirely to the topic of the liturgical arts. Following

---

8. Wilson, 7.

9. Two brief but useful sources of information on the subject of liturgical design consultants are Christine Reinhard, "Hiring a Liturgical Consultant," *E&A: Environment and Art Letter* (June 1993) 44–45, and Richard S. Vosko, "Liturgical Design Consultants: Who Are They and What Do They Do?" *Faith and Form* (3) (1997) 27–28.

10. The National Conference of Catholic Bishops devotes two paragraphs of its *Built of Living Stones* to the issue of liturgical (design) consultants. Article 199 of the document states that parishes involved in the construction or renovation of sacred buildings "should obtain the services of specialists in liturgical design." The document further stipulates that "the responsibility of the liturgical consultant [is] to assist the pastor, staff, and the entire parish with continuing education about the importance, role, and value of worship, and the impact of the church building upon worship." The consultant is also said to be responsible for assisting the architect in applying "the principles and norms of liturgical design to the practical and liturgical needs of the parish being served" (no. 200).

11. The brainchild of Ralph McInerny, this publication has a decidedly antiquarian character. The May–June 1997 edition, devoted entirely to church architecture, offers a series of articles and personal commentaries whose common theme is the inappropriateness of modernist design to the liturgical arts. Almost

an editorial statement that called into question the personal morality of today's church designers, an essay by historian James Hitchcock isolated one nationally known consultant/designer as an example of the "liberal Christians who think they have nothing of importance to tell the secular culture and that their proper role is to endorse the agenda of enlightened non-believers."[12] Professor Hitchcock's commentary was succeeded in turn by a column authored by his wife, Helen Hull Hitchcock, editor of *Adoremus Bulletin*, who counts the same consultant among the "New Barbarians" and "Iconoclasts" intent on robbing the church of its treasury of art and architecture. Being sure to note twice that the consultant was formerly a Franciscan priest, Mrs. Hitchcock offers an oversimplified explanation of his theories of design and compares him to the Pied Piper, who, the fable records, "was employed by the leaders of Hamlin but emptied the town of what it held dear."[13] In an article for *The Wanderer*, a publication that delights in thrashing those liturgical reformers whose views its editors consider at odds with orthodoxy, writer Paul Likoudis uses similar tactics to discredit the work of another well-known consultant/designer, a priest of the Diocese of Albany, New York, who has been assisting Catholic parishes for some twenty-five years. Rather than conducting an intrinsic critique of the consultant's substantial body of church projects, Likoudis instead takes him to task for the professional fees he demands, for his selective use of clerical dress, and for the style with which he presides at Mass—all of which contribute, the author concludes, to broader dissemination of the "Agony in Albany."[14]

For James Patrick, provost of St. Thomas Moore College in Fort Worth, Texas, the way to attack "the new liturgists" is apparently to denounce them altogether as persons misguided by their own hubris and intoxicated by the power they hold over simple believers. "It is heady stuff to be a liturgist," Patrick writes:

> . . . to be given the task of changing the piety and behavior of hundreds and thousands of people who do not see as clearly as the liturgist does. . . . It is heady to see through the old philosophies which spoke of reality, and to know that one, born perhaps in Poughkeepsie, or even New York, has gotten beyond Plato and St. Thomas. It is heady to have a part in destroying a liturgy two

---

to a person, the authors represented in this publication are suspect of most of what goes on today in the name of liturgical-architectural renewal and advocate a return to styles of church design that predate modernism, which they view as incapable of bearing sacred meaning.

12. *Catholic Dossier* (May–June 1997) 60.

13. *Catholic Dossier* (May–June 1997) 61–62.

14. "Catholics Weary of Illicit 'Changes' Bitter Over Church Renovation Plans," *The Wanderer* (March 26, 1992) 7.

thousand years old on behalf of a brave new ecclesiastical order. It is heady to be in the know and in power.[15]

Regrettably, public commentary such as this only heightens the animus that persists in the Church between opposing sides in the liturgical debate and does little to contribute to a sounder appraisal of the artistic and pastoral value of present-day church architecture. It is one of the unfortunate realities of our time that we Catholics have turned the hallowed ground of sacred ritual itself into a battlefield, whereupon we sacrifice each other for the sake of momentary, rhetorical victories. We have transformed ourselves into factions of temple guards—literally *fanatics*—each zealously protecting what it perceives to be the true and exclusive access to the *fanum*, the Sanctuary. Distracted by our infighting, by arguments over whether statues belong in churches or not, over the location of the tabernacle, over the very shapes and styles and decorative handling of our buildings, we have lost sight of the larger and more important issues that face us as a people that builds for the purposes of regular, solemn, and corporate worship:

- Given our immersion in a national culture that seems to have dispensed altogether with the notions of community and public space, are we even capable today of maintaining a concern for architecture that promotes communal experience among its users and makes clearer their interdependence?

- Given that we have ceased to be primarily a pedestrian culture, a nation of walkers, but have become instead a people dependent upon the automobile and thrilled by the freedom it provides us, are American Catholics capable of maintaining in architecture our sense of local, parochial identity or the tradition of slow and deliberate ritual procession to and from our centers of worship?

- Given our technocultural bent for compressing all sensory experience into the confines of a two-dimensional viewing screen and for the instantaneous transmission of information between anonymous parties, are we still capable of savoring collectively ritual gestures that require both spatial and temporal magnification?

- Given the increasingly *in*formal character of public behavior in our culture, are we capable of maintaining habits of worshiping and building that revel in *formality* and celebrate that which is planned, articulated, and ritualized?

15. "From Prayer to Politics: Minge, Michel and Monica Hellwig," *The Latin Mass* (Fall 1995) 37.

- Given the increasingly frigid emotional state of our culture, are we any longer able to be touched by the beauty and poetry of buildings put to sacred function?

The essays presented here, written over a period of about a decade, are an attempt to address such questions in a serious and studied manner and to offer some practical suggestions to the pastors, architects, and lay committees presently involved in the difficult work of church-building and renovation. My assumption is that success and failure in the realm of contemporary liturgical architecture are determined in the earliest stages of building projects, not at their conclusions. What has diminished the quality of much that we have erected in the last half-century is not so much our inability to draw or calculate well, or even to construct things that last. (On a purely technical level, we are probably as skillful as church-builders of any age have been at transforming architectural ideas into built form, and our comprehension of structural science is actually *superior to* that of the builders who have preceded us.) What is lacking today, I am convinced, is a clear sense of *why* we build; ours is essentially a theological problem, not a technological one. We wish desperately to build from belief—belief in our God, in the efficacy of our rites, in the power of art to reveal to us something about the divine. But it is precisely in the area of belief that we seem so often to stumble and lose our way.

In one sense, the challenge set before us to create an environment for Roman Catholic liturgy authentic to the needs of the Church in the United States is more difficult today than it was even a few decades ago. The pioneers of the first, or "experimental," phase of post-Vatican II liturgical design (ca. 1965–75) at least had a solid tradition *against which* to react as they sought to devise novel architectural forms to serve a *Novus Ordo*. Their inspiration came from two contemporaneous sources: the official statements of the Second Vatican Council and the accumulated body of modernist design theory that had had an influence on the work of painters, sculptors, and architects worldwide for roughly a century. For persons involved in the second, or "formulaic," phase of postconciliar church design (ca. 1975–85), the trick was to seize upon certain liturgical arrangements that worked well and to replicate them to the point of establishing a new canon for Catholic architecture appropriate to our time. (One thinks instantly in this regard of buildings conforming to the immensely popular "fan-shaped" plan, complete with sloped floors, natural wood ceilings, and an obligatory skylight above the sanctuary.) More recently, in our current "reflective" or "reactionary" phase of liturgical art (ca. 1985–present), the teachings of both the council fathers and of the inventors of modernism have undergone serious reappraisal, leaving some architects to doubt the very theological and aesthetic principles on which they have built entire careers. Having struggled hard to create buildings befitting the "Church in the Modern World"[16] proposed by Vatican II, the custodians of liturgical design now face a situation in which the concept of modernity itself, with its elevation of the new over the old, has become problematic. We are, in the minds of a great many interpreters of Western culture, well into a postmodern, post-Christian age, one in which the verities of even the recent past grow more ephemeral by the minute. In the ideological free-for-all that prevails, the faithful ask with honest confusion, *"Whose* Catholicism are we to embrace? *Whose* notion of what constitutes art that is suitable for sacred service?" These are questions that no *Universal Catechism* or style guide to church design is likely to put to rest any time soon, and one wonders whether, in today's complex and demographically heterogeneous Church, consensus can be achieved on anything but the most rudimentary components of a creed.

Despite the unpleasantness of the moment, however, it would be sheer arrogance for us to presume that we are the first generation of Christ's followers to face the challenge of comprehensive change in the social order. As the liturgist H. A. Reinhold made clear decades ago in his advancement of modern liturgical renewal, two impulses have emerged in every historical era that the Church has weathered, "one preserving what exists and the other striving along new paths." Such is not only nature's way, Father Reinhold argued, but is rather a condition that reveals the heart of Jesus himself, "[who] . . . used two parables to illustrate the growth of the church: the parable of the mustard seed indicating slow and regular growth; the parable of the leaven, illustrating the internal upheaval, the turmoil, and the explosiveness of change."[17] It is for us who claim a Catholic identity to determine how these opposing tendencies are best balanced, of course. And in being true to the natural dynamism that runs through both sacramental and artistic expression in the Church—one form of embodied prayer succeeding another, one corner of the City of God erected new as another is torn down—we must face squarely the possibility that the contributions of our *own* generation to the treasury of sacred art and architecture may in time be superceded by forms that are thought to be more intelligible to a future Church. There is much that we have learned from a quarter-century of liturgical and architectural experimentation, some of it by sheer blunder and by realization of our frequent short-sightedness. One likes to think that the kind of

16. The Church's sense of its own relevance and contemporaneity was expressed most explicitly in the council's landmark document, *Gaudium et Spes* (Pastoral Constitution on the Church in the Modern World, 1965), which challenged the faithful to act as agents of God's love, compassion, and grace in a world traumatized by sweeping cultural and technological changes.
17. *The Dynamics of Liturgy* (New York: Macmillan, 1961) 86.

indiscriminant destruction of church buildings that commonly happened in the 1960s and 1970s has given way to greater judiciousness in our treatment of them. Gone as well, one hopes, is the urgency with which we once tried to make Catholic architecture assume the complexion of the contemporary, commercial landscape, thinking that by so doing we could link it more literally to the sanctifying miracle of the Incarnation. Far from making places of worship more "transparent to the divine," however, the latter trend often succeeded only in making sacred realities less visible to human eyes. What we have come to understand, perhaps, is that religious buildings that are indistinguishable from their surroundings do not more readily infect the secular landscape with the sanctity they possess; they simply make the sacred all the more difficult to discern when it does reside in our communities.

From where we stand, at a historical moment sufficiently distant from Vatican II, one is able to survey both the wonders and the wreckage that we have produced in the name of liturgical-architectural reform—the latter possibly in greater quantity than the former. The final word on Catholic architecture has not been spoken, however, and it is difficult for the more optimistic of us not to see in the new millennium a vast and open platform of opportunity, upon which the Church will continue to assemble an array of places for the commingling of God and God's people. "*This* is the day the Lord has made" (Ps 119:25), the psalmist proclaims. It is into *this* age, *this* historical moment, with all its apparent difficulties, that we have been inserted by our Creator. We do not occupy our allotted space and time alone but are accompanied, Scripture tells us, by a divine Paraclete. Faith thus dictates that we persist in our exuberance for the day, in our openness to the mystery and wonder that are inseparable from the creative act itself, and in our conviction that the Spirit of God surely animates our work as builders of sacred places, guides it, blesses it, and inhabits it as well.

PART ONE

1

BEAUTY, HOLINESS, AND LITURGICAL SPACE

As a consultant to Catholic parishes involved in church-building or renovation projects, I am frequently asked to explain the goals of today's reform of sacred architecture. My response is succinct and echoes the Church's own directives on liturgy and its physical setting: We are challenged to create places marked by grace, places in which the sacred is clothed in forms both simple and compelling, places that unify worshiping assemblies and heighten their awareness of the multiple ways in which Christ is present in ritual actions. Our intent is not to erect grandiose and lavishly ornamented buildings, which are really beyond the means of most Catholic communities. Grandeur can burden good design under its weight, ornament can obscure it; and both, cheaply imitated, produce environments that are garish, overblown, and inauthentic. Neither is spectacle our intent, for little happens within our church buildings, frankly, that can compete today with the packaged displays of pyrotechnics offered us elsewhere. (Hollywood, NASA, and people at Disney, Inc., long ago conspired to break the Church's monopoly on special effects.) No, it is grace we seek, which is the proper goal of any Church bound to Christ.

Rarely is grace spoken of in connection with contemporary liturgical architecture, even by members of the various design professions helping the Church to reconfigure its places of worship. Yet the term is an appropriate one, and the fact that historically it has been used to describe experiences both of sense and of spirit reminds us of the alliance between beauty and holiness—*venustas et sanctitas*—that forms the very basis of Catholic art. Beauty, after all, is a gift offered us in courtship by a God anxious to claim our senses. It is redemptive, restorative, and, as the clinical research of psycho-therapist Rollo May suggested, "soul-baring."[1] So rare a thing is beauty that our impulse may be to savor it privately, stingily, in modest portions. Like the Eucharist, however, real beauty asks to be consumed whole, its effects increasing as it is shared communally by its beholders. Beauty in liturgical art and architecture results when expressive materials die to themselves only to be reborn in settings that serve the Church's highest form of prayer. Consciously or not, it is the Resurrection we celebrate each time we build a church, and by its beauty that we mock death itself.

The Church's Teaching on Beauty

The importance of beauty as a condition of the liturgical environment was spelled out in the Constitution on the Sacred Liturgy of Vatican II. The first article alone of the constitution's chapter on sacred art and furnishings contains three references to the beautiful in artistic expression, which it defines as an earthly manifestation of God's own "infinite beauty" (no. 122).[2] The constitution stipulates that places of worship and their contents ought to be "worthy, becoming and beautiful signs and symbols of the supernatural world" (no. 122) and instructs ordinaries to rid church buildings of artwork that is mediocre or pretentious (no. 124). "[S]trive after noble beauty rather than mere sumptuous display," the constitution notes, "[a]nd when churches are . . . built, let great care be taken that they are well suited to celebrating liturgical services . . ." (no. 124).

Further explanation of beauty's role in sacred places is found in the *General Instruction on the Roman Missal*, which encourages church-builders to work toward "noble beauty" not "ostentation" (no. 279). The threefold function of liturgical buildings—to promote participatory worship, to instruct the faithful, and to surround worshipers in an environment of beauty—is outlined in article 253 of the Instruction:

> For the celebration of the eucharist, the people of God normally assemble in a church or, if there is none, in some other fitting place worthy of so great a mystery. Churches and other places of worship should therefore be suited to celebrating the liturgy. . . . Further, the places and requisites for worship should be truly worthy and beautiful, signs and symbols of heavenly realities.

1. *My Quest for Beauty* (Dallas: Saybrook, 1985) 20.
2. Unless otherwise noted, all texts/translations of official statements are from Elizabeth Hoffman, ed., *The Liturgy Documents: A Parish Resource* (Chicago: Liturgy Training Publications, 1991).

Beauty that can "both inspire and reflect" (no. 18) is prescribed for church buildings by *Built of Living Stones*. "The external and internal structure of [a] church should be expressive of the dignified beauty of God's holy people . . . ," this instruction insists, as well as the sacred rites celebrated within them:

> Liturgical art and architecture reflect and announce the presence of God who calls the community to worship and invites believers to raise their minds and hearts to the One who is the source of all beauty and truth. Art and architecture that draws more attention to its own shape, form, texture, or color than to the sacred realities it seeks to disclose is unworthy of a church building for the liturgical action (no. 44).

Beauty and Architectural Space

How such principles of design are to be translated into actual places of worship has been left to local faith communities and the creative professionals who assist them. First among the concerns of any building or renovation team, however, must be the space itself that will serve worship, not the decorative treatment of the surrounding edifice, its symbolism or overt "sign value." I mention this having watched parish groups discuss in detail everything from the color of a church's carpeting to the shape of its façade without any consideration of the underlying liturgical plan. Absent from these discussions was the understanding that buildings—religious or otherwise—are more than mere stage settings or backdrops for human activities. They are complex networks of spaces bound by walls, floors, and ceiling planes that exert a subtle but real influence on those who inhabit them.

To design our sacred buildings well, we must remember that architecture is primarily an art of spatial problem-solving and expression, a near cousin of choreography. Architects take seriously the three-dimensional spaces people occupy in the built environment and hope to affect human behavior by means of the elements that define and illuminate these spaces. To architect Frank Lloyd Wright, space was nothing less than "the reality of a building,"[3] its essence and reason for being. Anyone who has ever passed through the public concourse of one of the country's great, historic railroad stations, sat on the front porch of a sprawling, Victorian mansion or simply curled up with a good book in the coziest room in one's own home might well agree with Wright's conclusion. Spaces sensitively designed engage us with a beauty that is inherent

---

3. Wright was fond of making this claim, which appears, among other places, in his *The Future of Architecture* (New York: Mentor, 1953) 28.

Fig. 1—Laurentian Library, Florence, Italy (1523–52). Michelangelo. *Ricetto* interior with staircase.

not applied, and their artistic authority is measured by the degree to which they make us feel and act as we might not otherwise.

Visitors to Florence's famed Laurentian Library, for example (figs. 1 and 2), a building designed by Michelangelo, encounter two spaces distinct in character and long admired for their affective power. The *ricetto*, or vestibule, is a dark, well-like cubical whose massive and exceedingly high walls press in around one. The library's reading room, on the other hand, amounts to a long corridor of light flanked by thin walls and many low-hung windows. Patrons

Fig. 2—Laurentian Library, reading room interior.

wishing to advance from *ricetto* to reading room must ascend an over-scaled staircase intentionally designed to confuse and disorient its users. What the architect (a Neoplatonist) achieves here is a three-dimensional rendering of the classic "Allegory of the Cave," in which one's progression from a place of darkness to one of light approximates the journey of mind and soul from ignorance to wisdom, illusion to reality, obscurity to clarity.

The power of architectural space to shape human emotions is apparent as well at a site like the Vietnam Veterans Memorial in Washington, D.C. (figs. 3 and 4), where visitors speak only in muted tones while processing down graded paths to the sunken vertex of Maya Lin's chevron-shaped masterwork. There, almost to the person, they are compelled to probe the monument's twin walls—like the Apostle Thomas probing the flesh of the resurrected Christ—and trace the names of beloved war-dead etched in stone. The ritual plays out daily without rule or instruction. Space alone dictates the human drama that unfolds in this abstract valley of catharsis.

Fig. 3—Vietnam Veterans Memorial, Washington, D.C. (1982).

What makes these examples of architectural design so instructive is that they do not depend upon applied embellishment or signage to make their points. (Lin's monument, in fact, is entirely free of decoration.) The respective

architects have resorted to the sparest expressive vocabularies, yet the effects of the spaces they have created are palpable. We who presume to build for the greater Journey and Memorial called "eucharist" should strive to achieve the same.

Fig. 4—Vietnam Veterans Memorial, detail.

The Evolving Space of Liturgical Prayer

Devising spaces capable of transforming us into a people of communal prayer is something we Christians have been up to for two millennia. In the course of Christian architectural history, many types of spaces have been pressed into sacred service, a fact often forgotten by those presently involved in building projects. At the very least, members of parish building or renovation committees should be familiar with the three conceptions of liturgical space that have had the greatest influence on Christian church-building: (1) the domestic space, (2) the basilican space, and (3) the modern, centralized space. Knowledge of these spatial models may prevent us from repeating the errors of our predecessors and free us literally to build upon their successes.

1. The Domestic Space

We know that it was in simple domestic settings that Christians first broke bread together in accordance with Christ's own mandate. The home was the centerpiece of family life in the ancient Mediterranean, a place where blood relationships and civic rapport between neighbors were rehearsed with care. What more fitting location could there have been for gatherings of God's adopted sons and daughters—especially during periods of acute persecution—than in rooms rich with familial associations?

The *atrium* at the heart of most Greco-Roman dwellings of the apostolic period provided space adequate to the needs of local churches as they assembled for inspired words and song. The *triclinium*, or dining room, with its tightly bound arrangement of reclining couches and banquet table, was the fitting place for the paschal meal. The relatively modest scale of these rooms, even within the house-churches maintained by wealthier Christian communities, lent the rites an air of intimacy. Christ himself was at once the mystical landlord, housekeeper, and table leader of every *domus ecclesiae*. To him clung a community of believers set adrift from the world by their baptism.

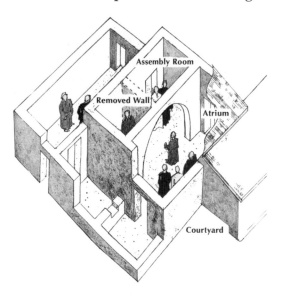

Fig. 5—Early Christian House-Church at Capernaum (First–Fourth Century).

Archaeological remains of early Christian house-churches at Capernaum (presumably the home of St. Peter; fig. 5) and at the Roman garrison town of Dura-Europos, Syria (fig. 6), suggest that the communities who used them felt free to manipulate the physical aspects of their makeshift chapels to improve the conditions for worship. At each of these sites, interior walls were removed and rooms conjoined to expand the liturgical space. The structural fabric of a church building was apparently of little consequence to our Christian ancestors, who saw it simply as a servant of the true dwelling of God—the baptized assembly.

2. The Basilican Space

Different in every way from the domestic meeting places of Christianity's infancy were the monumental edifices the Church began to erect in the fourth-century and continued erecting for the next sixteen centuries. Residential architecture may have been adequate to the needs of a third-rate mystery cult, disenfranchised from the world and unattached to its real estate. It hardly befitted a popular success, however, which is what Christianity became during the reign of Constantine the Great, first by imperial edict and thereafter by imperial association. Forced to acquire new accommodations for its corporate services, the Church seized upon a building-type known throughout the territories of imperial Rome as a component of every civic architectural program: the basilica (fig. 7).

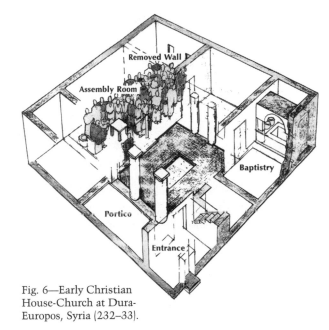

Fig. 6—Early Christian House-Church at Dura-Europos, Syria (232–33).

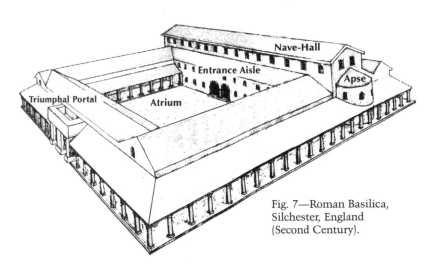

Fig. 7—Roman Basilica, Silchester, England (Second Century).

From the start, churches built on the basilican order imparted a formality to the rites they housed and gave emphatic expression to the growing distinction in liturgical roles between Christian laypeople and clergy. Indeed, the interior plan of a Christian basilica (figs. 8a and 8b) was essentially bicameral, consisting of a long nave-hall terminated at one end by a semicircular apsidal precinct. Linking these respective sites of lay and priestly action, but self-contained within a screen of wood or stone parapets, was the *schola (cantorum)*, or choir stall, reserved for an exclusively clerical ensemble of singers. Apse and *schola* together formed the strictly delimited liturgical core of the building, presided over by the local bishop and his presbyteral attendants. The open and more expansive nave acted as a general-purpose room for large and increasingly passive lay congregations. The whole was conceived as a vast, longitudinal pathway to the Heavenly Jerusalem, symbolized by the geometry and décor of the apse. The likeness of Christ, rendered in elaborate frescoes or mosaics, literally hovered over this *via sacra*, filling the faithful with awe and trepidation. Whatever intimacy Christians had previously enjoyed in their places of worship was now lost, diffused by the vastness of the complex and by a compartmentalized floor plan shaped more by ecclesial *polity* than piety.

3. *The Modern, Centralized Space*

So enduring was the basilican model of liturgical space that it remained the basis of Catholic church design up to the time of the Second Vatican Council. In the United States, for example, architects of the 1940s and 1950s knew exactly what kinds of buildings would please their Catholic clients. The floor plan was a given, an inflexible template into which the requisite parts of a church building were fitted like parts of a familiar puzzle. Architectural "pro-

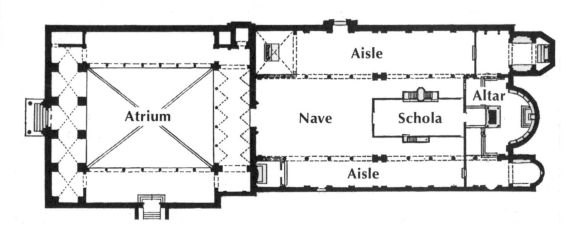

Fig. 8a—Basilican Church of San Clemente, Rome, Italy (Fourth Century, rebuilt, 1099–1108.)

Fig. 8b—Basilican Church of San Clemente. Interior detail with *schola*.

gramming," as we know it today, was virtually nonexistent, for the essential program for *all* Catholic churches had been established long before by the Council of Trent (1545–63).

Despite the immense popularity of basilican-type churches, however, they possessed an inescapable limitation: They could not facilitate the kind of active lay involvement in worship that the church of the twentieth century had come to embrace. As early as 1903, for example, in his famous *motu proprio* on sacred music, Pope Pius X urged that steps be taken to secure for laypeople "a more active part in [worship], as was the case in ancient times" (*Tra le sollecitudini*, no. 5).[4] At midcentury Pius XII likewise emphasized in public statements that liturgy is the work of the entire ecclesial body of Christ and an opportunity for laypeople to become one "in mind and heart" with the clergy who preside (*Mediator Dei*, nos. 18, 199).[5] Not as "outsiders and mute onlookers" (no. 192) did the pontiff wish the laity to attend sacramental events but as active participants.

4. Washington, D.C.: National Catholic Welfare Conference, 1903.
5. Washington, D.C.: National Catholic Welfare Conference, 1947.

Modest experimentation with church design in the first half of the century laid the groundwork for what since Vatican II has been an all-out reworking of the Catholic place of worship. The postconciliar church building (figs. 9 and 10), with its centralized seating arrangement and modest decorative scheme, bears little resemblance to the large and opulent structures of the past. Its interior space is focused upon the primary poles of liturgical action, and its outward appearance is more likely to be inspired by current trends in secular design than by the contents of a sacred pattern book. Architectural elements that previously fractured the worshiping body (altar rails, chancel screens, elongated nave spaces) have been discarded altogether, so that local groups of Christians may now sit down at table in spaces truly conducive to communal worship.

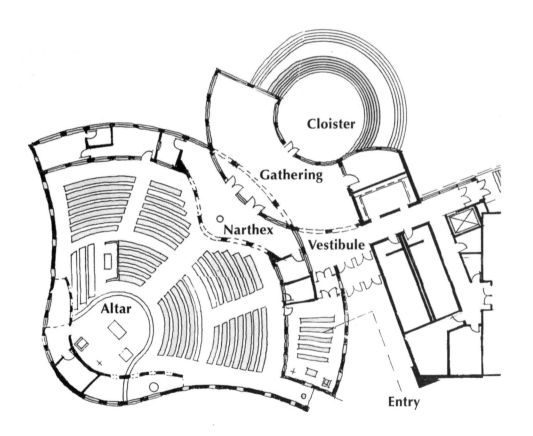

Fig. 9—Post-Vatican II Centralized Church. Our Lady of Grace Church, Greensburg, Pennsylvania (1999). Plan.

Fig. 10—Our Lady of Grace Church, Greensburg, Pennsylvania. Interior.

The Present Challenge

If it is true that every house represents a self-portrait of its occupant, then the House of God's People, ever under construction, must feature some element that reflects the faith of Catholics at the threshold of a new millennium. Finding the means to express religious faith through architecture proves particularly difficult in the United States, I believe, because the prevailing culture shows so little deference toward beauty, holiness, and place. The churches American Catholics build today must unfortunately fit into an architectural landscape populated increasingly by what former Yale art historian Vincent Scully has called "buildings without souls."[6] Gone are the noble edifices in which the populace once learned the lessons of history and the simple rules of civility. In their places stand the flashy buy cardboard-thin buildings of the commercial strip and the ubiquitous shopping malls. Pop culture now dictates public decorum, the mall is its classroom and shrine. If men now think it

6. "Buildings Without Souls," *New York Times Magazine* (September 8, 1985) 43, 62, 64, 66, 108.

acceptable to dine in restaurants without removing their hats, if movie-goers talk with abandon in theaters, if friends of bridal parties think nothing of roaming without hesitation through every corner of a church sanctuary, camcorders in hand, it is precisely because Americans have lost their sense of place and of place-related behavior.

How, then, are we who uphold the uniqueness of place to compete with the noisy hype of our surroundings? *We aren't.* Rather, our sights must be fixed steadfastly upon things that endure. We must be the world's memory of what beauty looks like, what sanctity feels like, and how both, when wedded in architectural space, can transform the human psyche. My comments do not flow from naïve idealism. I have witnessed within the competitive and often mercilessly cynical realm of architects and designers the wide attention paid recently to small and better crafted religious buildings (Fay Jones's Thorcrown Chapel in the Ozarks, Norman Jaffe's Gates of the Grove Synagog on Long Island, Tadao Ando's Church of the Light in Osaka, Japan, for example). A humble and authentic spirit is a virtue in architecture as in life, for it forces architects to weigh carefully every design decision they make. Smallness can arrest the attention of those weary of the gigantism that marks so much contemporary architecture. "Good things come in small packages," goes the cliché. So, sometimes, do holy and precious things, like the Church, which stands to benefit more today from buildings that speak with the clear and simple voice of the prophet than with the haranguing of the sideshow barker.

2

CATHOLIC SACRAMENTALITY
AND THE REFORM
OF SACRED ARCHITECTURE

When parish building committees, pastors, and architects meet to plan the construction or renovation of a place of worship, it is rare that they devote attention to so weighty a topic as "Catholic sacramentality." More often than not these groups quickly find themselves preoccupied with the many practical aspects of such an undertaking, leaving little opportunity for discussion of the unique character of the Church's rites. Yet it is only with a sensitivity to the natural alliance that exists between sacramental and artistic expression in liturgy that parishes can hope to realize the reform of sacred art and architecture envisioned by the Second Vatican Council.

Certainly one of the defining features of Catholic Christianity is the conviction that God's grace may be encountered by people of faith through means that are tangible, or sensible. When Catholics gather in worship we reveal most explicitly our identity as a people nourished by the Father, through the priestly mediation of Christ, in a manner that accommodates the sensate nature of our humanity. In liturgy it is the Church's particular habit to perceive actions, objects, and surroundings with sacramental vision, confident that it might give concrete form to its love of God and receive by the same concrete means the gift of God's salvific love. So it is, to the Catholic imagination, that a ritual bathing in water marks one's entry into the community of faith, an exchange of nuptial rings and solemn promises unites a man and a woman, and by the consumption of a eucharistic meal believers are made nothing less than human temples of the Living God. Through such acts Catholics imitate a Christ who, Scripture tells us, applied healing mud to the eyes of a blind man, washed the feet of friends, and once, in the face of protest, welcomed the anointing of his own body by a servant woman. Regardless of the particular characteristics of any sacramental act, however, whether it involves water or oil, or bread and wine, it is by its sacred design a vehicle of communication: Men and women offer themselves to God in their imperfect humanity, and God responds by sharing with this church a glimpse of God's perfect divinity.

Given the Church's reliance upon sense experience in the worship lives of its people, we are not surprised that historically it has employed the fine arts—music, the visual arts, dance, and drama, as well as architecture—as an ally to sacramental activity. For in art, as in sacrament, human beings seek to give form to the Formless. Like the sacramental action, the act of artistic expression mirrors the Incarnation itself, Christ's becoming the "visible image of the invisible God" (Col 1:15). Artists in the service of Catholic worship thus share in a special ministry, likened to the priesthood, that requires on their parts acts of sacrifice and "consecration." In their hands raw materials become something more than themselves; they become, like elements employed in the Church's formal sacraments, pathways to the divine. For architects and the various parish building committees with whom they collaborate, this implies a profound responsibility, since it means that the structures they devise must not function merely as neutral grounds of worship. Rather, buildings for Catholic celebration should participate in the very sacramentality that defines their reason for being. They must point beyond themselves, as all sacramental objects do, but simultaneously heighten the encounter between God and God's Church. This is not achieved through clever manipulation of stylistic or formal conventions, however, but can only result from sound design grounded in liturgical function. Competent designers thus realize that the unity of the worshiping assembly is the proper intention of any architecture that hopes to serve such action.

Numerous writers have noted that it is precisely the physicality of sacrament and art, the aesthetic content of both, that helps preserve the Church's experience of the sacred from "the temptation of becoming ethereal."[1] When the Church's faith is embodied in sacramental-artistic form, when it assumes an objective aspect through some sensible word, gesture, or object, the faithful are made stronger in their belief. This is so because of the reciprocity inherent in every sacramental event, for sacraments at once arise from and are sustain-

1. Anthony Padovano, "Aesthetic Experience and Redemptive Grace," in Gloria Durka and Joanmarie Smith, eds., *Aesthetic Dimensions of Religious Experience* (New York: Paulist, 1979) 3.

ers of the faith of a prayerful community. The Constitution on the Sacred Liturgy describes the sacramental process in this way: "[Sacraments] not only presuppose faith, but by words and objects they also nourish, strengthen and express it; that is why they are called 'sacraments of faith.' They do indeed impart grace, but, in addition, the very act of celebrating them disposes the faithful most effectively to receive this grace in a fruitful manner, to worship God rightly, and to practice charity" (no. 59). Likewise, the Bishops' Committee on the Liturgy have reminded Catholics in the United States that "[p]eople in love make signs of love, not only to express their love but to deepen it," in a statement evocative of the Epistle of James:

> Love never expressed dies. Christians' love for Christ and for one another, and Christians' faith in Christ and in one another must be expressed in the signs and symbols of celebration or they will die. . . Faith does not always permeate our feelings. But the signs and symbols of worship can give bodily expression to faith. Our own faith is stimulated (*Environment and Art in Catholic Worship*, no. 9).

By recognizing the reciprocity at work in sacraments, their roles as both objective expressions and objective sustainers of faith, we better appreciate the problem that can arise should changes occur in their outward forms. If Catholics truly are instructed and fortified by the sacraments they celebrate, it follows that any significant revision in the form of sacramental ritual—such as that initiated by Vatican II—might effect a corresponding shift in the very faith of the Church. We know from experience that the same holds true for those sacred arts that have traditionally assisted liturgical piety. A reshaping of their formal characteristics is a matter of considerable importance, because it signals either a fundamental change in the Church's beliefs (*what* it expresses) or a change of the manner in which the Church wishes to convey its beliefs (*how* it expresses). In either instance, such revisions in the sacred arts may be accompanied by a degree of ambivalence as Catholics struggle to determine what is essential to their faith and how best to communicate these tenets through the language of art. Catholics would do well, however, to embrace this struggle as a good and necessary one, for, as Susan Roth has noted, "[b]oth the aesthetic and the sacramental make their effects felt through symbols, and the symbols in turn need constantly to be reinterpreted in light of their ability to speak to the spirit of the time."[2]

Much of the discomfort associated with the liturgical-artistic reforms of our time may well stem from Catholics having forgotten what it means to be spiritual pilgrims. After all, during the four centuries that the Council of Trent

2. "The Aesthetic and the Sacramental," *Worship* (November 1973) 516.

provided the model of ceremonial propriety, the Church became comfortable with the external magnificence and seeming immutability of its rites. The cost of this illusory comfort was the Church's memory of having once been a people consumed in self-discovery, journey, and mystery—the requisites for both sacrament and art. The unfortunate consequence of the liturgical excesses of the Tridentine Church was a skewing of the alliance between sacrament and art, the effects of which were felt in Catholic ritual practices up to the time of Vatican II. And in the United States, where the religious sensibilities of an immigrant church were shaped as much by new-found prosperity as by its Baroque inheritance, art's deference to sacramental intelligibility also proved an unlikely prospect. Throughout the nineteenth and twentieth centuries, hardworking ethnic parishes in all parts of the country could rightly boast of their ability to imitate the grand style and settings of familiar, Old World liturgies. For their parts, lay Catholics were not displeased with a tradition of architectural design that distanced them from the events of the sanctuary, as there was much in the typical parish church building to intrigue the senses while the presiding priest performed his secret, canonical routine.

As late as 1951, however, critics of architectural designs that fulfilled the demands of Church polity over those of corporate prayer could complain of "little apparent unity of purpose or evidence of deep understanding among the millions of Catholics who attend Sunday Mass" and an "untold number of churches in which the liturgical aspect of the Eucharist is relegated to an unimportant place."[3] Those observers who looked most critically at Catholic church architecture in America in the decades before Vatican II lamented the popularity of "romantically 'mystical' and darkened interiors,"[4] which were intended by designers partly to transport Catholic clients from the unpleasantness of their workaday lives. "Anyone who has studied the church buildings of recent decades," wrote Maurice Lavanoux at midcentury for *Architectural Record* magazine, "cannot fail to sense the fact that a romantic association with the shadow of past achievements vitiated much of the work produced."[5] Others sensitive to the proper role of architecture in the service of Catholic worship echoed the sentiments of musical pedagogue Justine Ward, who argued that "Christian art, like other art, is perfect only through perfection of form; but Christian art is opposed, more than all other arts, to the display of form."[6]

3. Daniel Coogan, "Let the Faithful Hear the Mass," *America* (February 17, 1951) 585.
4. Maurice Lavanoux, "Recent Trends in Catholic Church Design in America," *Architectural Record* (April 1939) 81.
5. Lavanoux, 79.
6. "The Reform of Church Music," *Atlantic Monthly* (April 1906) 461–62.

Today, with renewed interest in sacramental theology and recognition of the primacy of the assembly in liturgical action, liturgical designers are encouraged by the Church's official legislation to strive toward "noble simplicity" in their works and to avoid "ostentation" (*General Instruction on the Roman Missal*, no. 279). In its *Environment and Art in Sacred Worship*, the American Bishops' Committee on the Liturgy similarly describes the contemporary setting of Catholic worship as modest in scale and hospitable: "It does not seek to impress, or even less, to dominate, but its clear aim is to facilitate the public worship and common prayer of the community" (no. 52). Likewise, a directive on church-building and renovation from the Diocese of Columbus, Ohio, recommends that architects, pastors, and lay committees "seek function first" and "beauty rather than display."[7] "We are not concerned with building monuments," the directive states:

> Do not seek to impress but only to express the spirit and function of the worshiping Mystical Body. When this is done well, wide attention will accrue to the work. . . . Noble beauty results when simple materials are used well. Extravagant materials and out-dated styles which defeat the economics of modern construction should be avoided. We are building for a pilgrim church.

Members of the architectural profession generally have been earnest in their attempts to comply with such prescriptions and, in so doing, to make Catholic liturgy more inclusive of the users of their buildings. The simple, open, and unified interiors that characterize modern Catholic church buildings give witness to an aspect of sacramental action that heretofore enjoyed little architectural magnification, namely, the role of the assembly as living sacrament of Christ to itself and to the world. Ideally, worshipers experience Christ's own friendship in each other and are bolstered in their faith by an architectural environment that relieves liturgy of its historic anonymity. In the most successfully planned buildings, God's love is hardly imagined as flowing from some literal "channel of grace." Instead, it is felt to pervade a pool of persons acquainted with grace from baptism, whose entire environment is rightly identified as "sanctuary."

Whether this ideal can ever become the norm for the Church's architectural practice in the new millennium remains to be seen. There can be no doubt, however, that in the ongoing development of building forms that are responsive to the needs of the renewed liturgy, those persons responsible for liturgical design will take continued inspiration from the alliance of sacrament and art and from the Church's own intention to stand before the world as a living sign of Christ's nearness to all people.

7. Office of Liturgy, Diocese of Columbus, Ohio, "A Summary of the Letter and Spirit of the *Constitution on the Sacred Liturgy*, the Instruction for the Implementation of It, the *Notitiae* of the Post Conciliar Commission, and recent conferences concerning Construction and renovation of Churches," (n. d.) 1.

3

THE PASTORAL DIMENSION
OF CHURCH RENOVATION

Few events in the life of a parish priest prove more daunting than renovation of his community's place of worship. Not even the erection of a new church edifice, which requires pastors and their associates to become at once fundraisers, project supervisors, and chief apologists of liturgical reform, matches the difficulty of modifying an existing structure. Building from the ground up can at least entice parishioners to dream of *what might be* and to anticipate the gleaming novelty of everything that will enter into their new facility, while renovation causes them often to dwell solely upon the demise of *what has been.* It represents for many Catholics a profound loss, a relinquishment of surroundings perceived to be familiar and true, no matter how inadequate they may be to the worship needs of the contemporary Church. Like Moses guiding Israel through the desert, then, priests who initiate church renovation projects must be prepared to suffer the inertia of those in their charge content to stay put rather than to search long and hard after a place where communal worship might be improved. It is prophetic work these priests assume, which, more than money or talent or energy, requires absolute conviction on their parts that what they are doing is right.

The correctness of the Church's liturgical-architectural renewal was made plain by the fathers of Vatican II, who defined it as one of the clergy's chief duties and a goal to be pursued with "zeal and patience" (Constitution on the Sacred Liturgy, nos. 14, 19). In the midst of the council, Pope Paul VI himself instructed priests to implement "wholeheartedly and loyally" the liturgical changes of the day (*Motu proprio* on Sacred Liturgy, 1964, introduction).[1] Statements from a distant see, however, offer American pastors little defense against the noisy protest and controversy that typically arise with first rumor that they intend to update an old and cherished building. "Popes and councils come and go, but this is *our* parish," an angry laywoman reminded me recently at the conclusion of an adult education session, suggesting that Roman ordinances had no bearing on such strictly local matters as how Catholic parishes worship or where. There persists among many of the faithful, in fact, the notion that the entirety of postconciliar reform has been wrong-headed and part of a demonic plan for the wholesale undoing of Catholic culture. (This sentiment is shared by at least one critic of my own contributions to the reform of church architecture, whose anonymous, serialized letters to me close with the exclamation, "Viva Michelangelo, Raphael and Leonardo!") As respondents to a survey I conducted in one parish argue, "God himself is offended by all the changes we're making in the church":

> The purpose of the Mass is to concentrate on the Body and Blood of Our Lord . . . designs for church renovations should not deprive us of this experience or put too much emphasis on "community," which is secondary. . . . We don't want our historic churches modernized. . . . We wonder what God thinks when he looks down on what we're doing.

In large and small parishes across the United States, what historian Thomas Bokenkotter has called "the myth of the unchangeable Mass"[2] holds fast. Worse, it seems, than reminding Catholics that they constitute a Church of sinners (as the Bishops' Committee on the Liturgy does so candidly in its *Environment and Art in Catholic Worship*)[3] is to insist that they are no less a Holy People called to worship in ways that foster corporate unity. The latter might require them to change the places in which they regularly celebrate the sacraments and, in turn, to dig as deeply into their pockets as they must their souls.

Few priests find it easy to request so much from their parishioners. Fewer still are eager to enter into the exhausting committee work that is today an inescapable part of any architectural endeavor. Those who do, however, seem to share several common traits that set them apart from their peers. Generally,

1. In Austin Flannery, o.p., ed., *Vatican II: The Conciliar and Post Conciliar Documents* (Collegeville: The Liturgical Press, 1984) 42.
2. *A Concise History of the Catholic Church* (Garden City: Doubleday, 1977) 224, 392.
3. Article 36 of this statement acknowledges that "[t]he Church is a church of sinners, and the fact that God forgives, accepts and loves sinners places the liturgical assembly under a fundamental obligation to be honest and unpretentious, without deceit or affectation, in all it does."

they are mature, self-possessed men in their fifties and sixties, old enough to remember the exhilaration of Vatican II yet more youthful in their thinking than today's average seminarian. They are men comfortable with their priesthood who, despite the prevailing air of liturgical confusion, find meaning and personal completion in daily celebration of the Eucharist. Though attacked as "church-wreckers," "radicals" and destroyers of Catholic tradition, rarely are they careless with the patrimonies of parish churches entrusted to them. Most act with great deliberation, knowing full well the weight that each of their decisions carries. If they err during a renovation procedure, it is usually on the side of conservatism; seldom do the buildings they modify break new artistic or functional grounds on their way to improving Catholic worship. They are, in short, leaders of a church in transition who readily admit that the architectural reforms they implement are but temporary solutions to larger, systemic problems that may take us decades to remedy.

Rarely do we hear the stories of priests who renovate church buildings, though each, I believe, has something to do with pastoral courage. (The stars of today's published accounts of renovation projects seem always to be the artists, architects, and consultants whose reputations are common knowledge among members of the sacred art crowd.) Thus it is fitting for me, as part of this collection of essays devoted to the remaking of Catholic church architecture, to relate the experiences of three representative pastors with whom I have been fortunate to work in my capacity as a design consultant. My intent is not to heroize these priests nor to suggest that they enjoy a special aptitude for the architectural process. They are simple men who define their priestly ministry primarily in terms of service to others, and it is their concern for the liturgical prayer of others that compelled them to enter into the murky waters of church renovation. They are priests who learned by *doing*; the aim of this essay is to inspire other pastors who might *do by learning*.

Msgr. Bruce Allison, St. Mary Church, Meadville, Pennsylvania

"Ours was not a model project," admits Msgr. Bruce Allison, former pastor of St. Mary parish in Meadville, Pennsylvania.[4] "It wasn't systematic or tidy. . . . We had no money in the beginning, and I didn't know where we'd find it." Allison recognized the need for architectural renovation immediately upon arriving at St. Mary Church as pastor in 1983, however. The parish's small,

---

4. Msgr. Allison, who, for several years after completion of the St. Mary Church renovation, was headmaster of the Cathedral Preparatory School in Erie, Pennsylvania, currently pastors Erie's St. Mary of Mount Carmel Church.

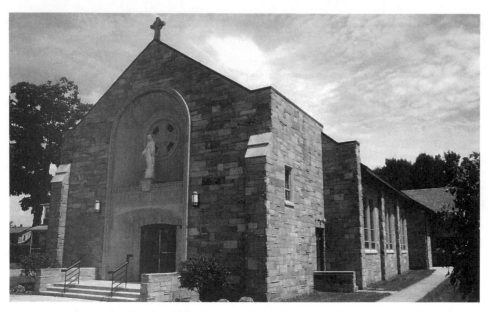

Fig. 11—St. Mary Church, Meadville, Pennsylvania (constructed 1955; renovated 1994).

vaguely Gothic church building (figs. 11 and 12), erected in the mid-1950s, was in need of extensive structural repair; its roof had suffered water damage and the exterior stone walls needed repointing. Of equal concern to the pastor was the unhappy condition of the building's interior, which, among other things, required new paint, updating of the electrical system, and a thorough reworking of the liturgical plan. Modest changes to the space following Vatican II had reoriented the altar of sacrifice but left it stranded within a deep, rectangular sanctuary. The latter was strictly divided from the nave by an imposing arch and a marble communion rail. "I never enjoyed presiding at Mass in that space," Msgr. Allison notes, "because I felt so far from the people."

Other components of the parish's physical plant were in more immediate need of attention, unfortunately, forcing the pastor to defer any work on the church until 1989. At that time Allison issued a call to the parish for persons interested in learning more about liturgical renewal and its architectural implications. Some thirty parishioners accepted this invitation and, under Allison's personal guidance, began studying the popular writings on eucharistic prayer by Rev. Eugene Walsh, s.s. Later, as there emerged from this group a smaller and more clearly defined "Aggiornamento Committee" charged with renovation of the worship environment, written catechetical resources were supplemented by films, videos, and firsthand analysis of sacred structures throughout the diocese that had already undergone the process.

Parish-wide catechesis was an important goal of the pastor, as well. At one point in the project, for example, Allison devoted nearly a dozen, consecutive weekend sermons to the topic of sacred liturgy. These were coordinated with the contents of educational materials distributed to all parishioners as they gathered for weekend services. Aware that homilies are generally to be reserved for the explication of sacred Scripture, Allison nevertheless felt that routine liturgical instruction from the pulpit was essential to the success of the project. "To make any renovation work," he explains, "you've got to get the people to share the vision of worship put forth by Vatican II. If they aren't caught in the dream, the project will fail." Allison knew that popularizing "the dream" in this ethnic (predominantly Italian-American), working-class, and fiercely traditionalist community would be among his hardest tasks.

Behind the scenes, and initially with little guidance from diocesan agencies, Fr. Allison proceeded to address more practical matters, including the setting aside of funds with which to pay for the eventual renovation. Having no personal experience with architectural problem-solving, he sought the assistance of a religious furnishings studio that offered a full range of design services. (In the beginning, however, no architect was engaged for the project.)

Fig. 12—St. Mary Church, Meadville, Pennsylvania. Interior before renovation.

Lengthy discussions with representatives of this firm resulted in several schematic designs for the renovated church, none of which Allison or his committee found particularly exciting. A diocesan building commission likewise dismissed the designs as dated and uninspired. This served only to frustrate the progress of the project and compound Allison's fears that he was squandering precious time and monetary resources. Deliberations with the diocese also made the pastor more acutely aware of the scrutiny of his clerical peers. He notes in retrospect, "I could feel the pressure of my [fellow priests] . . . and didn't want the rest of the presbyterate to look down on me or on our project."

In 1992, fully three years after beginning the journey toward a renovated place of worship, Msgr. Allison retained the services of a liturgical consultant

Fig. 13—St. Mary Church, Meadville, Pennsylvania. Interior after renovation.

and an architect. Under the direction of these professionals, the work of the Aggiornamento Committee gained both clarity and momentum, and individual committee members began to appreciate more fully the liturgical implications of their discussions. By the autumn of 1993, the committee was able to share architectural renderings of the proposed renovations with the entire parish community. To the delight of the entire building team, the renderings were generally well received, and the project entered into a speedy design-refinement phase. Actual renovation of St. Mary Church was begun in June of 1994, and the project was completed nine months later. The structure was formally rededicated by Most Rev. Donald W. Trautman, Bishop of Erie, Pennsylvania, in December of 1994.

Fig. 14—St Mary Church, Meadville, Pennsylvania. Nave interior from bema.

In its revised form (figs. 13–15), the building's interior plan allows an assembly of two-hundred worshipers to gather on two sides of a bema platform that is thrust into the nave. The primary liturgical appointments are fashioned in part from marble veneers salvaged from the original sanctuary and are easily visible from anywhere in the nave-hall. A large, wood screen, whose trabeated form is reminiscent of ancient, European shrines and temples, separates the newly established Blessed Sacrament chapel from the site of liturgical action. The whole is treated to a new lighting scheme, a combination of fixed pews and flexible seating, and a color palette that brightens and unifies the interior.

Fig. 15—St. Mary Church, Meadville, Pennsylvania. Eucharistic reservation chapel.

"I like worshiping in the new space," says Fr. Allison. "In fact, I like just *being* in it. Sometimes, in the afternoon, I'll just go into the church and sit there looking at the light, the forms and colors." Though Allison appreciates the beauty of the renovated church, however, he is not blind to certain weaknesses in its design: a hollow bema platform that is noisy to walk upon, a new heating system that may have been too expensive, a baptismal font whose design does not accommodate the immersion of adults.[5] And the priest is not anxious to undertake such a project again. "It takes too much out of you," he concedes. To fellow pastors who must renovate churches, however, he offers these concrete suggestions: (1) "Question everything," (2) "Don't be intimidated by architects or contractors," and (3) "Keep your sights fixed on the fundamental reason for your work, which is prayer."

Rev. John Fischer, St. Matthew-in-the-Woods Church, Summit Township, Pennsylvania

The weeks surrounding Easter 1993 will likely never be forgotten by Rev. John Fischer, former pastor of St.-Matthew-in-the-Woods parish in Summit Township, Pennsylvania.[6] Months earlier, Fischer had initiated a project to update the interior of a small, free-standing chapel central to the history of his parish, and, as Easter neared, he looked forward to the project's timely completion. On the eve of the last Sunday in Lent, however, literally minutes before he was to preside at an anticipatory Mass, Fischer's dream of a swift, efficient, and uneventful renovation procedure came to an end. As the priest tells it, he was preparing to celebrate the Eucharist when a member of the parish approached him, clipboard in hand, requesting permission to circulate a petition against the renovation. Startled by the interruption of his pre-Mass preparations and preoccupied with the many tasks at hand, Fischer summarily dismissed the parishioner and denied his request. This served only to incite a group of like-minded parish members who hoped to turn local opinion against any plans of tampering with the sixty-year-old structure.

Throughout the week that followed, popular opposition to the project intensified, prompting Fr. Fischer to call emergency meetings of the renovation committee on Palm Sunday and Good Friday. The committee members were unanimous in their decision to see the project through to completion but feared that opponents might grow more militant. These fears were realized on the evening of Easter Monday, when anonymous threats against the pastor

---

5. With the influx of young families into the parish, the font design is under reconsideration. In the first year after renovation of its liturgical setting, St. Mary Parish grew by more than fifty families.
6. Fr. Fischer is currently pastor of St. Lawrence the Martyr Church in Albion, Pennsylvania.

were telephoned to the rectory and a contractual meeting involving the project architect and contractor was disrupted by a contingent of angry parishioners. Events took their strangest turn, however, when renovation opponents mounted a campaign through local news media and radio talk shows to embarrass the pastor publicly. Fischer, whose work had gone on quietly and with-

Fig. 16—St. Matthew-in-the-Woods Church, Summit Township, Pennsylvania (constructed 1936; renovated 1994).

out opposition for the better part of a year, now found himself embroiled in a public debate that extended beyond parochial boundaries and painted him as either saint or scoundrel.

At the center of the controversy was a quaint, stone chapel erected in 1936 by St. Matthew parishioners themselves on the site of an existing frame building (figs. 16 and 17, see fig. 17 on page 50). Known locally as the "Stone Church," the chapel stands on the edge of a semirural, wooded parcel and is a popular attraction to religious pilgrims, sightseers, and wedding parties. Bus loads of out-of-town shoppers, straight from excursions to a number of nearby shopping malls, regularly visit the chapel as well. For the people of St. Matthew parish, the structure provides a setting for weekday liturgies and for two services each weekend. Because of the chapel's modest seating capacity (it accommodates only 115 worshipers, even after renovation) it is perceived as ancillary to the parish's primary worship place, a large, multifunction hall. Nevertheless, the chapel and its contents hold important associations for parishioners that are at once religious, historical, and familial.

Fr. Fischer's reasons for wanting to change so revered a building are not beyond understanding. Years of unchecked eclecticism had left the Stone

Fig. 17—St. Matthew-in-the-Woods Church, Summit Township, Pennsylvania. Interior before renovation.

Church's interior volume crowded with an incongruous array of liturgical and devotional fixtures. No less than a third of the floor plan was consumed by a chancel and polygonal apse, leaving the nave somewhat cramped and unconducive to the ritual movement of its users. So narrow was the processional aisle, in fact, that communicants at funerals found it difficult to pass by the casket on their way to receiving Holy Eucharist. The circulation of Communion processions was frustrated further by a poorly proportioned chancel arch that sprung from points well within the building's side aisles. (It was not uncommon for taller parishioners to strike their heads on the underside of this element when returning to their pews after receiving Communion.) Pews and floor tiles were worn and dangerous, as was the electrical system. Overall, the church's once rustic charm had given way to a shabbiness that paint alone could not mask. Through renovation, Fischer hoped to improve the physical conditions for worship and dispel a spirit of negativity that had pervaded the parish for years.

With considerable support from the local chancery, Fr. Fischer proceeded with his plan and saw the renovated church rededicated in the autumn of 1994. "I'm not usually an emotional guy," he confesses, "but in this place I become one." Indeed, Fischer recalls numerous incidents in which he and other worshipers have been deeply affected by the chapel's modified design. "A visitor came up to me and told me that this was the first church he'd been in that seemed to encourage him to sing, that *encouraged* him to participate in the Mass. Well, this guy was responding to the sense of intimacy and focus that this place generates." Fischer adds that he has noticed greater participation in liturgy among the people of the parish themselves since completion of the chapel renovation.

St. Matthew's original, bicameral interior has been transformed by reconfiguration into a tidy, unified whole (figs. 18–20; see color insert for figs. 19 and 20). Reorientation of the liturgical plan has put the altar, ambo, and presidential chair along one the building's side walls. These are bracketed by movable chairs that have been ganged together to form several sections. A major, processional pathway has been retained on the plan's longitudinal axis, and is terminated by a tabernacle island. The chapel's handsome scissor trusses and matrix of rafters and purlins are accented by a lighting scheme that illuminates the ceiling, while the floor of the building enjoys a new, slate surface.

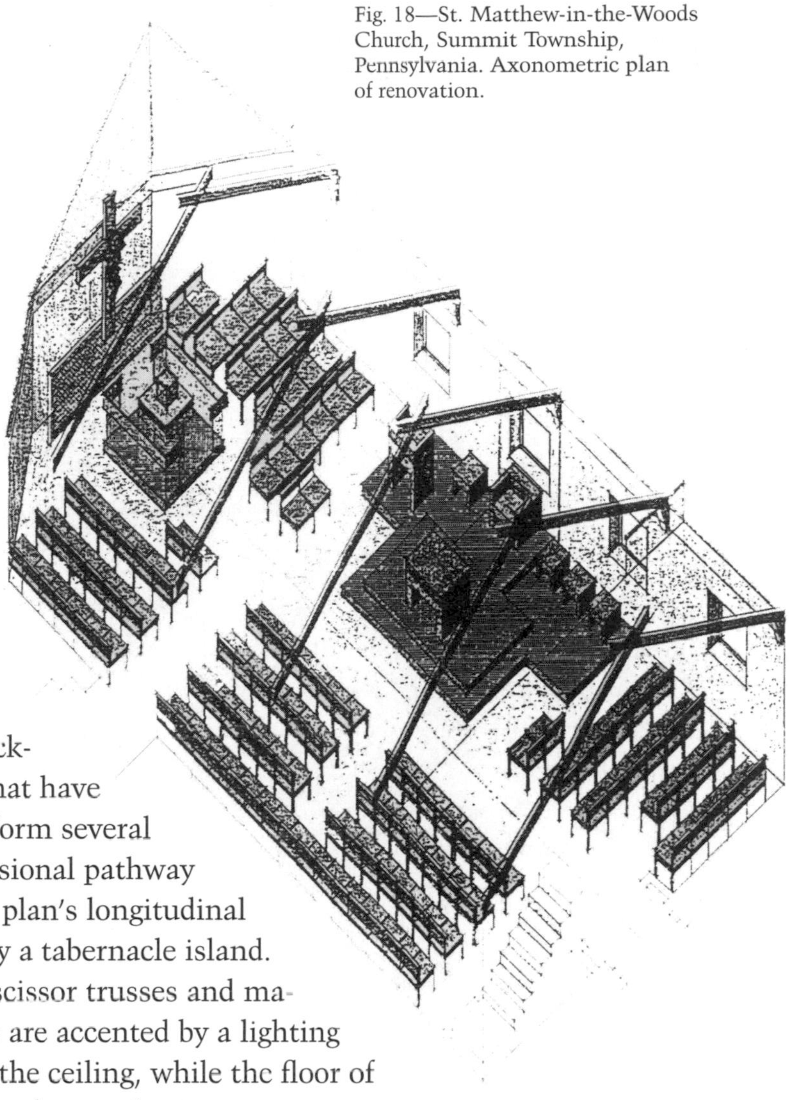

Fig. 18—St. Matthew-in-the-Woods Church, Summit Township, Pennsylvania. Axonometric plan of renovation.

Several St. Matthew families have chosen to leave the parish rather than accept the chapel's renovated state, a fact that Fr. Fischer laments. He remains convinced, nonetheless, that his actions were pastorally sound and guided by a concern for the liturgical life of the entire community. Perhaps most disappointing to the priest is his realization that parishioners did not avail themselves in great numbers of the education and discussion sessions that prefigured actual renovation of the Stone Church. Some of the loudest criticism of the project in fact came from persons who had chosen *not* to attend public presentations made by the pastor, architect, and liturgical consultant. "Y'know," Fischer concludes, "some Catholics just don't want to learn more about the changes to our worship. But, if I had just one suggestion to give to other pastors in my situation, it would be simply this: Educate! Educate! Educate!"

Msgr. Charles Kaza, St. John the Baptist Church, Erie, Pennsylvania

When Msgr. Charles Kaza[7] was appointed pastor of St. John the Baptist Church, Erie, Pennsylvania, in 1985, the large, neo-Romanesque church building (figs. 21 and 22) maintained by his community was already nearly ninety years old. Typical of Catholic places of worship dating from the early twentieth century, the church rose from a vast cruciform plan, its interior spaces neatly distinguishable from each other by form and function: nave and transepts for the activity of up to 500 lay worshipers, chancel, apse, and ancillary chapels for priestly confection of the Eucharist. Applied to the building's wall surfaces was a rich pastiche of painted and sculpted decorations; the shafts of its massive, nave columns, fashioned from plaster, were treated to faux-marble finishes. In the sanctuary and chapels stood marble altars built into elaborate reredoses in the Italian Baroque style. Stained-glass windows bearing in German the names and aspirations of the parish's founding families completed the scene.

Fig. 21—St. John the Baptist Church, Erie, Pennsylvania. Exterior.

By the time of Msgr. Kaza's pastorate, however, St. John Church had lost much of its original beauty and was plagued by serious structural and mechanical problems. As Kaza began to address the latter, he realized the necessity for a comprehensive renovation plan, one that would grow organically from the parish's liturgical needs. Analysis of the circulatory habits of Mass at-

7. Msgr. Kaza, pastor of St. Tobias Church in Brockway, Pennsylvania, is currently Episcopal Vicar for the Eastern Vicariate of the Diocese of Erie, Pennsylvania.

tendants, for example, revealed that many entered and exited the church through secondary doorways, never pausing to interact with worshipers who chose to use the processional portals and assemble in the building's central nave space.

St. John was a building perfect for worshipers who wished to remain anonymous. Such persons simply passed its major entrance and moved with haste to the ranks of pews that abutted its side walls. From there they could gaze obliquely at the crowd in the nave but remain partially hidden by a screen of columns. In effect, the church served two liturgical assemblies simultaneously, one that filled the nave and one that hugged the lateral walls.

The primary impulse of the pastor and renovation committee, then, was to eliminate from the building those features that worked against the corporate unity of worshipers or prevented them from functioning as intimate partakers in the events at the ambo and altar. A lengthy "vision statement" prepared by the committee was emphatic on these points:

> We recognize that the plan of our church reflects the clerical, ritualistic climate of the universal church prior to the liturgical [reforms] of 1963. . . . The present configuration of pews presents both visual and physical barriers. . . . The design of furnishings and their location . . . further speaks to a division between presider and faithful. We envision a space which fosters a unified, simple community conscious of all its members as embodiments of Christ, celebrating knowingly, actively and fruitfully together as one.

Fig. 22—St. John the Baptist Church, Erie, Pennsylvania. Interior ca. 1945.

Sensitive to the needs of those parishioners who feared change, Msgr. Kaza decided to proceed slowly and deliberately with work at St. John. Considerable attention was directed toward adult catechesis, which included in 1992 a lenten educational series built upon the topic of corporate prayer. Attempts to keep the entire parish informed of the status of the project culminated in two, back-to-back, town hall meetings, at which schematic designs and a three-dimensional model of the renovated building were unveiled. The latter proved particularly useful in conveying to those not accustomed to reading architectural drawings the scope

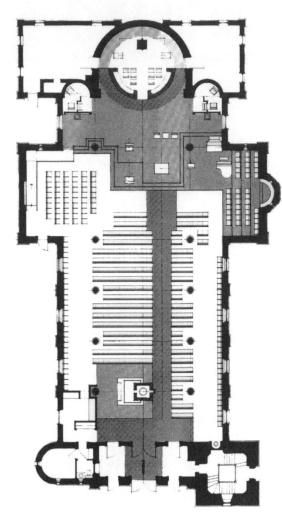

Fig. 23—St. John the Baptist
Church, Erie, Pennsylvania.
Renovation plan.

of the project and the spatial relationships between the church's interior parts
that would result from renovation.

Throughout the nine months that St. John was undergoing physical
change, the parish worshiped in the church basement. The intimacy of this
setting, composed as it was of movable chairs encircling a centralized altar, was
appealing enough to lead some parishioners to lament their eventual move up-
stairs. What the parish encountered when the church was reopened for the Vigil
of Christmas 1993 was a place whose basic geometry had remained intact but
whose functional core was wholly transformed (figs. 23–25; see color insert for
figs. 24 and 25). Having been liberated from the chancel, the altar ambo and
presider's chair now stood virtually at the building's crossing, beneath a refur-
bished groin vault. Flexible seating for members of the choir and other lay worshipers filled the transepts, while new pews straddled a processional aisle in the
nave that had been moved off the building's major axis. Worshipers entering the

church through the main set of doors discovered two parallel axes of importance, one that ran through the heart of the church and terminated at a tabernacle in the apse, another defined by a processional aisle whose terminus was the altar of sacrifice (see plan, fig. 23). A massive, semicircular parapet-bench standing between tabernacle and altar further established a distinction between the respective areas of private and corporate action. A large baptismal font and immersion basin were situated near the entrance bay-gathering space, a powerful reminder of the parish's baptismal identity and historic patron.

Msgr. Kaza was pleased with the results of the project, though he vividly remembers the sensation he had upon entering the church at the outset of actual renovation. "The building had already been torn up, it was gutted, and my only thought was, 'What are we *doing*?' The project was a moment of grace, though, and despite the occasional moments of anxiety and the sleepless nights, I had no doubts that it would definitely make worship better around here." Kaza notes further that the real test of the renovation's success was the way in which the building performed during its first Triduum and Easter Vigil services. He cautions fellow pastors who renovate that the work they undertake will inevitably shake "the rock of peoples' faith." "Invest in a good educational process," he adds, "and select a committee that is hard-working, open-minded and aware of the complexity of the issues involved in this work."

Conclusions

There comes a time in every church renovation project when the pastor overseeing it is confronted simultaneously with the grandest and most mundane of problems. While worrying about such heady matters as, say, the fate of the Roman Catholic Church and the future of sacramental prayer as we know it, he must remember to keep the church doors unlocked for the contractors or to help prospective brides find suitable settings for their weddings—anywhere but in his church. He must remember that the subcommittee on stained glass meets every Tuesday night for the next month and that pews with kneelers will cost the parish considerably more than those without. He must remember the subtle shades of difference between walls painted in stone colors, white or gray, and an endless variety of floor coverings. Most of all, perhaps, he must remember that in the midst of the confusion that seemingly affects every aspect of parish life for the duration of "The Project" there will be passing glimpses of grace and beauty intended to sustain him. These will come, as divine gifts inevitably do, when least expected—with the generous monetary gift of an anonymous donor, with a note of encouragement from a parishioner, with first sight of the new gathering space or altar or font. Rarely are the "messes and miracles" of our faith more real or more intimately connected than when we disassemble an existing place of worship only to build anew in a different form.

There is agreement, at least among the priests cited in this essay, that the weariness one is left with upon completion of a church renovation project in time gives way to personal satisfaction and pride in the knowledge that one has done something tangible to improve a small corner of the church's earthly residence. In the early decades of the twentieth century, a generation of priests saw to the development of religious properties—schools and churches, rectories and convents—all of which were signs of both personal and parochial ambition. To the generation of priests that has come to maturity since Vatican II now falls the responsibility of making these properties usable to Catholics who little resemble their predecessors. The challenge remains the same: to erect from nothing and with limited resources places in which the Church's love for God and God's love for the Church are joined in sacred action.

In an age when terrorism, urban violence, and natural calamity so often destroy the fabric of public buildings, we Catholics persist in building up an architecture of praise and thanksgiving. It is, in words once used by author John Gardner to champion the art of literature, a heroic struggle we enter into, "a game played against chaos and death, against entropy."[8] We build because we cannot do otherwise, convinced as we are that God directs our industry and is more concerned with renewing the face of the earth (Ps 104:30) than with obliterating it. We should renovate just as easily, certain that the outward appearance of sacred buildings themselves is ultimately of less importance than the faithful who inhabit them.

To the priests who lead this work the Church turns for strong leadership and a sense of direction. More than this, though, I think lay Catholics hope to detect in their pastors at least some measure of confidence that all is not wrong with the way the Church currently prays or sings or dances or builds. The charge is a great one and frequently requires of individual priests a good bit of play-acting. No greater is it, however, than the charge of standing surrogate each day for the Christ who would have us all be fashioned into living temples of his spirit. This is the pastoral dimension of church-building and renovation—one that must not be overlooked as the Church continues to remake the physical accommodations for worship.

8. *On Moral Fiction* (New York: Basic Books, 1978) 6.

4

LET'S STOP RENOVATING
CHURCH BUILDINGS
*(AND START RENOVATING
THE CHURCH)*

Once, years ago, when my younger brother and I were just boys, we got it into our heads to waste the better part of a perfectly beautiful summer day in the basement of our house, tearing apart some old orange crates we had found. The darkness of the basement often concealed our mischief, which, on this occasion, involved the crates and a set of expensive woodworking chisels that hung above our father's workbench. The latter were part of a collection of tools much prized by our father and displayed with care like trophies on a pegboard-wall. Ritual objects, really, their value lay as much in the attractiveness of their shapes, the way they felt in the hands, as in the work they helped accomplish.

But "ritual" wasn't what the two of us were after, and the shiny tongues of metal seemed just right for digging nails from orange crates or prying their frames apart. Banging the blades from behind with hammers worked best, we discovered, though frequently we would drive one squarely into the spine of a nail or drop one head-first onto the concrete slab at our feet. The nicks and chips that began to multiply along their perfectly beveled edges were hardly enough to stop our noisy demolition work. And, anyway, we figured that if the chisels ended up where we had found them, no one would know they had been touched in the first place.

A father's eyes are more discerning, and when ours later discovered the damaged tools he acted swiftly and with uncharacteristic calm. Summoning us to the scene of our offense, our father made my brother and me watch as he painted a broad, red stripe across the length of the basement floor—a line of demarcation that henceforth divided his world of order and grace from the chaos of childish pranks. We were instructed never to cross this threshold and realized that we would not again handle for some time the dangling trophies that lay beyond our reach.

Years later, after childhood had given way to greater maturity, my brother and I were again summoned to the basement, this time to join our father in his special preserve. The painted line, now faint and dust-covered, had lost most of its power to repel us, and we now understood that its purpose had been to protect us from injury and our father's hand tools from misuse. With considerable ceremony our father invited us to draw close to his workbench, where, to our amazement, he proceeded to instruct us in the proper use of each tool that hung there. We learned their names and working parts, what their functions were and how they should be cared for. Together, the three of us bent down low to paint out what remained of the red stripe, and, in the course of an afternoon, our father's prized possessions became our own.

I have often reflected upon these personal "Lessons of the Basement" and thought them somehow related to the long history of Catholic worship, including the Church's most recent attempts to reform the style and setting of its corporate worship. For centuries, of course, we Catholics ran red lines of one sort or another through the hearts of our church buildings to distinguish the respective places of priestly and lay activity. Chancel arches, rood screens, altar rails, parapets, processional staircases—all contributed to the perceptible boundary that stood between the ordered stillness of the sanctuary and the popular commotion of the nave. Among the achievements of the Second Vatican Council, however, was an invitation to lay Catholics to cross freely the threshold barring them from full participation at their eucharistic tables and to receive with greater understanding the sacramental tools of redemption maintained there. Liturgy, the council fathers made clear, demands that all members of Christ's ecclesial body be able to see, hear, and act without obstruction, and the places reserved for liturgical prayer must be laid out accordingly.

Thus it was, in the decades immediately following Vatican II, that architectural elements designed to distance lay worshipers from ritual actions and objects were systematically removed from the liturgical environment, dismantled and painted over. The clergy's spatial refuge was invaded by increasing numbers of lay ministers eager to assist at sacramental celebrations. Whole assemblies of lay worshipers literally inched their way closer to the respective sites of oblation and proclamation, and the possibility existed that Catholics might begin to worship as unified bodies in unified buildings.

Sadly, however, the possibility of truly communal prayer in American Catholic parishes has remained only that, and while much has been done to modify the forms and decorative complexions of our church buildings, comparatively little energy has gone to educating the faithful they serve. Across the country one encounters liturgy as staid and uninspiring as that maintained before Vatican II, performed in buildings that were supposed to have improved long ago the Church's liturgical practices. It is not inappropriate, then, to propose that American Catholics stop renovating and building places of worship—at least temporarily—until we have overcome the habits that make it so difficult for us to achieve excellence in sacred liturgy and art. In this essay I wish to identify three.

Pragmatism

There is a strain of pragmatism that runs as strongly through the American Catholic Church as it does the national culture as a whole. To be sure, we Catholics profess a creed that is patently *im*practical. It challenges us to love enemies, store our treasures in heaven, embrace the Cross. As commonly practiced in the United States, however, Catholicism amounts to fulfilling a minimum of religious prescriptions before getting on as quickly as possible with the business of "real life." (Consider the popularity of so-called "Quickie" or "Convenience Masses" available on Saturday evenings at most American parishes, the poor attendance by the faithful of any function not mandated by canon or custom, the frantic race to the parking lot that eclipses the Concluding Rites of our eucharistic celebrations, and so on.) Between great expanses of time given to worldly matters we squeeze short excursions into the realm of the sacred, just often enough to gain some diversion from the banality of the streets.

Not surprising, then, is the difficulty many American Catholics have relating to the liturgists, artists, and architects who have thrown themselves into the work of reshaping the place of sacred worship. Such persons are, by choice or temperament, open to mystery; they know that creating the proper setting for ritual is less a calculated, assembly-line operation than a creative journey whose direction and outcome may defy prediction. This doesn't sit well with, say, members of a parish building committee eager to piece together a liturgical environment with the ease and thrift of catalog shoppers: some laminated wood trusses here, some mass-produced furnishings there, a splash of synthetic greenery or banner art for the walls, an institutional-size punchbowl at the front doors (for baptism, of course) and *voilà*—instant sanctity!

We skimp on what is considered peripheral to a parish's common piety only to cheat ourselves of the rich and challenging experiences that true liturgical prayer has always taken seriously. Tell parishioners that a plaster statue of the Sacred Heart is crumbling and they will gladly pay for its repair. Tell them it is the very manner and space of their worship that needs repairing and the checkbooks close reflexively. "If it ain't broke, don't fix it!" comes the refrain from opponents of architectural reform (as if the building practices of Catholic Christianity have not been fundamentally "broke" for centuries). Catholics simply will not embrace a cause they do not understand, and they do not understand, even at this late date, what the liturgical arts have to do with getting us all into heaven.

Language that Divides

Contributing further to the rift between promoters of architectural reform and those who wonder why Catholic churches have to be tampered with in the first place is the absence of a shared language. On the one hand there are the liturgically minded in every parish who are fond of casting their arguments in trendy, technical jargon; on the other, a segment of the Church that cannot put into words even the simplest tenets of the faith. The "liturbugs" (as they are sometimes called) rhapsodize over the importance of "gathering spaces," "worship spaces," and "places of reservation"; of "ambos," "ambries," "fonts," and "bemas," which, for all their historical and canonical accuracy, are terms that mean little to the uninitiated. Even words like "liturgy" and "Eucharist," considered to be common parts of Catholic speech, offer no grounds for meeting, as half of the Church continues to seek its salvation in "watching Father say the Mass."

Given this language gap, it is not uncommon for meetings between parish groups and liturgical design professionals to approach the anarchy of Babel. I recall one incident in which a young, intelligent but hopelessly soft-spoken architect was conferring for the first time with building committee members about the renovation of a parish church. The architect spun out marvelous theories about the remodeled building acting as "a metaphor for the unity of the parish" and a place where Eucharist would be central. At the end of his dissertation a woman blurted out: "You can change anything in the church you want to, but don't touch my St. Anthony [statue]. He's what I concentrate on during Mass, and I want to be able to touch his feet like I always do when I come back from Communion."

So much for "metaphors for unity."

Enter the "liturgical design consultant"—part artist, part catechist, part traffic cop. Many American dioceses require parishes that build or renovate to engage these relatively new members of the religious art profession, if only to coordinate the efforts of the scores of paid workers and volunteers involved in a modern building project. But consultants can contribute in their own way to the free-for-all that sometimes ensues when persons of varying agendas and levels of theological-artistic expertise collaborate on the creation of a church. Worse yet, they can stifle the free exchange of ideas that should accompany any architectural endeavor. Three tacks used by consultants achieve the latter: (1) the "Czarist Approach," whereby they impose their wills on clients and demand absolute deference in matters of artistic taste; (2) the "Rubricist Approach," whereby they require complete conformity with the letter of the Church's official directives on liturgy and art; and (3) the "Process Approach," whereby clients are kept occupied with endless "self-study," "imaging" or "visioning" sessions, "dialogs," surveys, town meetings, and the like. Each approach is based upon the presumption that the consultant knows what is best for his or her client. (I know of one consultant who holds such contempt even for the opinions of fellow designers that he refers to them as merely "tools.") Yet consultants often establish only a phantom relationship with the parishes they serve, and the decisions they make can affect the life of a community long after they have fled the scene. Those who suffer most are the parishioners themselves, who typically tire of the bullying and busywork and relinquish all responsibility for the design of their church to paid professionals.

Consultants do indeed provide a valuable service to the Church today, and their knowledge may well be the only thing that saves many parishes from ruinous attempts at church-building or renovation. Nevertheless, we should not forget that liturgical consultants of any kind are only essential to Catholic communities as long as the latter continue to treat liturgy itself as foreign territory, like tourists in some strange country requiring the assistance of guides or translators. Ideally, the Church should put the whole lot of consultants out of business (including this writer!) by instructing its members in the history, art, and practice of liturgical prayer. Given a common language with which to communicate and the skills to distinguish greater artistic expression from lesser, the faithful might begin to speak for themselves to the creative professionals they employ; and their church buildings will likely be more authentic expressions of their own parochial identities than of religious art brokers purchased for cash.

Warehousing the Sacred

Despite the efforts of Church leaders to convince us that liturgical buildings ought to function primarily as homes to human assemblies united in prayer, there persists among Catholics a strong impulse toward temple-building. Never mind the repeated scriptural warnings against trying to confine God's presence to the walls of an earthly edifice. Never mind the contents of the major legislative documents of our time, which characterize the place of Catholic worship as human-scaled, modest, and hospitable. What many of the faithful say they want are good, old-fashioned "houses of God," vast enough to enshrine the static, sacramental presence of Christ-in-tabernacle, the likenesses of various holy persons, and the accumulated mementos of a time before Vatican II, when everything Catholic rang with greater certainty. No other aspect of recent reform has proven more contentious, in fact, than the suggestion that we empty churches of everything obscuring Christ's presence in the baptized assembly. "The problem with all this renovation business," preservationists complain, "is that it's stripping our architecture of the very things that once made it distinctively 'Catholic.'"

The reaction is understandable. What used to differentiate places of Catholic worship in the United States from the meeting places of other Christian groups was the prominence of elements not directly related to the Church's official or liturgical rites (multiple tabernacles set into extravagant reredoses, armies of devotional statues, racks of votive lamps, painted and sculpted references to papal or episcopal authority, etc.). The requisite parts of a preconciliar building were worked into an eclectic mix of artistic forms and styles intended to convey at once the richness and antiquity of the faith. It mattered little that often the effect was only skin-deep, a product of glossy veneers, frothy plasterwork, gilt, and painted stenciling. There was still something more substantial to be experienced in Catholic buildings than in the plain, white boxes erected by Protestant communities. The American Catholic artistic sensibility arose from *horror vacuorum*, literally a fear of empty spaces and the Puritanism they engendered. So we crammed our churches to the rafters with overdesigned imitations of European splendor and reveled in our ability to outdo the Methodists, Baptists, or Presbyterians down the street.

If the reforms of Vatican II come hard to Catholics, it is precisely because we often behave as did Christ's first disciples, awe-struck by sanctuaries built by human hands but blind to the Living Temple standing in our midst. Having been driven since the Council of Trent to erect magnificent warehouses for the sacred, we are now encouraged to build up a holy people in whom God might dwell and to clothe it in an architectural mantle that is exquisitely simple, pure, and direct. Postconciliar legislation offers us an ecclesiastical equivalent to the architect Mies van der Rohe's famous dictum, "Less is More," which challenges our long-standing assumption that in prayer, as in life, the acquisition of *more* is proper, that *more* is holier, and that *more* is pleasing to our God.

Conclusions

Many suggest that the Church's pastoral leaders should persist in their attempts to change the style and setting of worship whether the majority of Catholics are prepared for change or not. Design influences human conduct, the argument goes, and by redesigning its sacred places the Church will inevitably cause the faithful to act and pray differently. What three decades of experimentation have demonstrated, however, is that even places of greatest beauty and liturgical propriety have no spell over persons not disposed to such things. At a town hall meeting I observed in one parish recently, for instance, an elderly opponent to a proposed renovation project proudly wore a sign around his neck that read: NEGATIVE SOUL. Throughout the meeting this gentleman sat glumly—coat on, frown fixed, mind clamped shut—unwilling to add his voice to the discussion at hand. There would be no "fuller and more active participation" in public debate by this Catholic, even less, apparently, in the liturgical rites of his parish. The sad fact is that such "negative souls" abound in the Church today, and their presence continues to frustrate the renewal of sacred worship and its related arts.

Clearly, the quality of buildings for worship is not about to improve until we are all convinced of worship's importance in Catholic life—and priests may be the first to need convincing. But the prospect of reeducating oneself as well as the entire membership of even a single parish is enough to scare many pastors into inaction. "I'd love to renovate our church building and improve liturgies in my community," a pastor once admitted to me, "but I don't want to provoke the people." What does it mean to pastor, however, if not to provoke and prod and otherwise cajole one's flock into following the truest course toward salvation?

Pastoring in the area of liturgy and the arts is something we have sorely lacked in the United States, which leads me to my initial proposal: Let us call a general moratorium on church construction and renovation projects in American dioceses for a period of several years, during which time the National Conference of Catholic Bishops (NCCB), through its organ, the Bishops' Committee on the Liturgy (BCL), could undertake a comprehensive effort to increase liturgical literacy among the faithful. Such an initiative could reach Catholics where they are captive, namely, at weekend Mass, and its agenda might include the following:

- Have the BCL produce a primer on sacred worship and art to be affixed to every missalette, prayerbook, and Mass guide that litters a pew in an American Catholic church. This publication could restate much of what was contained in the BCL's previous statements on liturgical music (1972) and environment (1978, 2000) but in language accessible to a broader audience.

- Have the NCCB mandate that all priests in American dioceses be capable of explaining the contents of the primer described above. At least one weekend a month during Ordinary Time could be devoted to liturgical catechesis in American parishes. Preaching on these weekends would address liturgical issues in light of the Gospel.

- Let diocesan liturgical commissions initiate a comprehensive inventory of Catholic properties in their respective territories. At the end of the building moratorium these commissions could encourage parishes with sacred environments insufficient to the demands of modern worship to renovate or rebuild.

There is no doubt that shoring up the "living stones" (1 Pet 2:4) comprising the human dwelling place of God will be vastly more difficult than fiddling with the bricks and mortar that make up our worship buildings. A comprehensive reform initiative will be costly and time-consuming. But when have expense or time been proper criteria for Christian action? When have true followers of Christ failed to proclaim the Gospel simply for fear that it would not bear instant fruit? To be Christian is to sacrifice oneself for things of ultimate importance. Liturgical prayer has such importance, the Church has stated publicly (Constitution on the Sacred Liturgy, no. 7). Now it is time to act upon these beliefs by renovating the people who fill the buildings we hold in such high regard and, in so doing, to transform from the inside-out the expanses in which our solemnest rites unfold.

5

COMING TO TERMS
WITH MODERN DESIGN

At a meeting of a parish building committee in which I participated recently, one of many planning sessions that would eventually lead to the construction of a new church edifice, the discussion centered upon liturgical furnishings. The committee members were already familiar with the basic footprint their building would assume. They had reviewed schematic designs of the interior, knew the location of doors and windows and how high the walls would stand. Now it was time to talk with greater specificity about the design of the major appointments. As design consultant to the project I asked aloud and in the most neutral way possible the questions appropriate to the occasion: "Given the rites your community will celebrate in this new structure, what characteristics should the altar, ambo, presider's chair, and baptismal font possess? How can the forms of these sacred fixtures best convey the identity of your parish and the faith of the Church universal?"

The response from the committee's self-appointed spokesperson was immediate. "We don't care what the things look like," he declared, "just as long as they're not *modern*. The people won't tolerate that." The remaining members of the committee nodded their heads in silent agreement, and I knew that as difficult as it had been to convince them to accept a building with a strikingly contemporary form, even harder would be the task of preventing them from filling it with all manner of clunky, "religious-looking" objects.

The tragicomic element in all this is that while American Catholics continue to recoil from visual art and architecture perceived as even remotely modern, the surrounding culture has entered into a phase of political-intellectual-artistic change that, for better or worse, has come to be known as "postmodern." (Among professionals in the art world, in fact, it has become fashionable to speak of modern art only in the past tense. Even basic art history textbooks now treat modernism as a phenomenon with a clearly defined chronology that begins in the mid-nineteenth century and ends roughly a century later.) In short, we are now twice-removed from the artistic currents of the day, having never come to terms with the modernist spirit that pervaded twentieth-century painting, sculpture, and architecture, and having more recently missed the emergence of newer and decidedly *non*-modern means of expression. "Give us liturgical art we can make sense of," the faithful clamor, which typically means something devised before the Industrial Revolution. Thus I fully expect that when the cultural history of the twentieth century is someday written, the largest Christian body in the world will be remembered as having rarely partaken of a living and timely art but persisting instead in stubborn historicism.

Catholics are not *supposed* to reject liturgical art in modern forms, of course. We belong to a community of faith described by Vatican II as one that offers "free scope" (Constitution on the Sacred Liturgy, no. 123) to artists wishing to serve sacred worship in new and experimental ways. Nevertheless, many in the Church maintain the belief that modern design is inherently unfit for liturgical service because it fails to evoke the memory of some earlier, nobler, or more pious age. The roots of the Church's enmity toward modernist art are complex and ultimately inseparable from its struggle with modernity itself. It is primarily a visceral phenomenon, however, not a cerebral one, for I suspect that few Catholics bring a studied response to the works of modern artists and architects. Fewer still are attuned to the serious theorizing that surrounds them. Catholics reject modernist art simply because it doesn't *feel* right, aesthetic theories be damned. The principles at work in modernism run contrary to a deep-seated instinct shared by many believers that, in liturgy at least, craves literalness, cohesiveness, and predictability. Modern art, which delights in fracturing conventional imagery and ways of thinking, appears to challenge too many of the assumptions that underlie the faith. In the words of art historian Leo Steinberg, who speaks for the art audience at large, it "invites us to applaud the destruction of values which we still cherish, while the positive cause, for the sake of which the sacrifices were made, is rarely made clear."[1] For American Catholics, modernism's per-

1. "Contemporary Art and the Plight of its Public," in Gregory Battcock, ed., *The New Art* (New York: Dutton, 1973) 216.

ceived threat to cherished values comes from at least three sources, and the sacrifices it demands are many.

1. Modernism's Threat to Tradition

From its birth in the nineteenth century, modern art has been explicitly revolutionary. It is an art comfortable with the flux and ambiguities that characterize life in a fast-paced, mechanized age. The term "modern" itself, derived from the Latin *modo* ("just now"), designates an art "just now emerging," an art of the immediate moment, not the past. Modern artists force their audience to the edge of psychic tolerance because they believe that only from the edge can the beauty of the fleeting moment be grasped. New and spontaneous creative acts breathe with vitality, modernists insist, while art that is bound to tradition and canons of propriety lies static and dead. "We rebel against the groveling admiration of old canvases, old objects," the Italian Futurist painter Umberto Boccioni wrote in 1910, in one of many so-called "manifestoes" that catalyzed early modernism, "and against the enthusiasm for everything motheaten, dirty, time-worn. . . . [We uphold] everything young, pulsing with life. . . . [We propose] to destroy the cult of the past, the obsession with the antique, the pedantry and formalism of the academies."[2]

Understandably, an institution as protective of its traditions as the Catholic Church has found it difficult to accept such valedictory intentions. Looking to the past is something we Catholics do reflexively, after all, as ours is a history rich in patterns for living established by prophets and kings, martyrs and saints—even a flesh-and-blood Messiah. What does the present offer us, many of the faithful wonder, but a chaotic existence in which moral patterns of any kind have all but vanished? Modern art challenges us to confront contemporary life on its own terms, however, one speculative step at a time. "It makes no laws," the late novelist and Chaucer scholar John Gardner once observed, "only very difficult, complicated suggestions":

> That's why [modern] art has so long been hostile to religion. It's not that artists don't believe in God or in religious principles . . . but that every individual religion has a rigid code, even if it's a loose code, like "Do what Jesus would do". . . then they tell you what Jesus would do. . . . [T]he problem is that religions always have simple answers which exclude people . . . they make nice, neat laws . . . . Art never does that.[3]

2. "Manifesto of the Futurist Painters," in Robert Goldwater and Marco Treves, eds., *Artists on Art* (New York: Pantheon, 1972) 435.
3. From Don Edwards and Carol Polsgrove, "A Conversation with John Gardner," *Atlantic Monthly* (May 1977) 47.

Gardner speaks for more than a few generations of creative talents who have been put off by the Church's compulsion to prescribe "nice, neat laws" for moral and artistic conduct. Authentic artists, the kind who believe that art's role is to transform the hearts and minds of its beholders, seldom thrive in an environment as hermetic as the one maintained by the Church. (Consider the plight of artists in any present-day totalitarian state, where, as in the Church, art is officially controlled and used as a tool of indoctrination. Their art grows shallow, rigidly formulaic and mechanical, or it simply withers from lack of fresh air and stimuli.) Sadly, of the countless artists who have served the Church, only a fraction are remembered by history as creative innovators, and nearly all of these were persons who questioned prevailing, ecclesiastical conventions. Indeed, what we learn from the nameless geniuses who invented Gothic architecture, for example, or from such Renaissance masters as Leonardo, Michelangelo, and Raphael; from Bernini, Caravaggio, and El Greco; from Georges Rouault or James Ensor or Henri Matisse; from the great, twentieth-century Rhineland architects Rudolf Schwarz and Otto Bartning is that art cannot be generated by formula. Rather, it arises from the type of sober introspection that makes life as difficult for its admirers as it does for its makers. Art is not for the faint-hearted, modernism argues, and neither should liturgy be if it involves participation in the very death and resurrection of Jesus Christ.

2. Modernism's Threat to Community

Modern art has never sought to be populist. From the start it has celebrated the ego of the individual creator, making no attempt to hide its disdain for all that is safe, conventional, and enjoyed by "the masses." To the modernist, life immersed in community means entrapment, because it demands sacrifice of personal autonomy and conformity to rules of behavior that may be arbitrary or outdated. Hence the nineteenth-century conception of the artist as an agonized misanthrope, part prophet, part lunatic. "Civilization is what makes [one] sick,"[4] the post-Impressionist Paul Gaugin contended. And, indeed, throughout the history of art, the mark of the artist's good health has often been detachment from the social group; the mark of his/her artistic virtue has been popular rejection.

It is said of modern artists that they wish not to communicate with everyone but only with those viewers sympathetic to their cause. The audience for modern painting and sculpture, therefore, has always been a rather

4. Quoted in Horst de la Croix and Richard G. Tansey, eds., *Gardner's Art Through the Ages*, 8th ed. (New York: Harcourt Brace Jovanovich, 1986) 869.

cultic one—literate, urbane, progressive. Modern architects, on the other hand, cannot presume such understanding from the range of persons looking over their shoulders. Architecture has no exclusive "audience," really, only users, most of whom today would gladly dispense with fancy theories and novel forms for roofs that do not leak, rooms that are not drafty, and building façades that are generally pleasing to look at. Architecture is an intrinsically overt and public art, even when it involves private funding and property. Every time an edifice is raised into place, people must make way for it and learn to live with it in their midst. Thus it has been the habit of modern architects to see themselves as heroic social engineers capable of improving societies by manipulating the physical environments they inhabit.

At important birthplaces of modern design, like Germany's famous Bauhaus (a school of art and technology active between 1906 and 1933), the art of building was regularly spoken of in lofty, metaphysical terms and practiced by students with monkish discipline. Walter Gropius, director of the Bauhaus for nearly two decades, likened the work of his institution to the cathedral-building projects of the Middle Ages, in which armies of skilled workers allied themselves in a single, all-encompassing enterprise. "Let us create a new guild of craftsmen, without the class distinctions which raise an arrogant barrier between craftsman and artist," Gropius announced. "Together let us conceive and create the new building of the future, which will embrace architecture, sculpture and painting in one unity, and which will one day rise to Heaven from the hands of a million workers, the crystal symbol of a new faith."[5] Gropius's "new faith" lay in the modern artist-as-world-builder, who, aided by innovative science and technology, would create an exquisitely rational and ordered dwelling place for humanity.

Such thinking has been lost on Catholics, who sense only that church buildings designed in the modern style are considerably more austere than those of the past. Gone from modern churches are the types of applied decoration that used to engage the popular eye, replaced by forms that seem too sterile to bear any meaning, religious or otherwise. What distresses Catholics even more, perhaps, is the implied arrogance of an architecture that seeks to dictate the lives of its users, however noble its aims. (Frank Lloyd Wright, for example, often argued that architects should give their clients what they *need*, not what they *want*. Wright himself was particularly good at telling clients what they needed and charging them handsomely for the service!)

---

5. From original text of the "First Proclamation of the Weimar Bauhaus" (1919), reproduced in full in Herbert Bayer, Walter Gropius, and Ise Gropius, *Bauhaus 1919–1928* (Boston: Charles Branford Company, 1959) 16–17.

Catholicism intends to build up not only holy persons but a Holy People. The sanctification it offers believers is achieved by the diminishment of self, by placing oneself at the service of others. The flaw in modern architectural practice, as many in the Church see it, is precisely that it puts the whims and creative intuitions of individual designers above the interests of common people, thus negating architecture's fundamentally servile role.

If the Catholics who today make up parish building and renovation committees treat architects with suspicion, it is, I believe, because they perceive them as belonging to an exclusive, professional clique—like modern doctors, lawyers, and other professionals—whose manners, goals, and even language are not shared by the general public. "Architects are so 'artsy,'" a Catholic laywomen once confided in me. "Half of the time you can't figure out what they mean by successful *spaces* or how buildings want to *become* something. . . . It's all double-talk, and it confuses the average person."

There is an element of truth in this, of course. Among the requirements for participation in the heady discourse that surrounds contemporary art and architecture is familiarity with their art-historical and philosophical underpinnings, and a willingness to forego preconceptions of what images or buildings should look like. Appreciation of modern art (like the artistic expression of any age) follows from understanding; and understanding, in turn, results from inquiry. Whether Catholics are at all inclined to undertake the remedial work that might lead to fuller comprehension of modern design remains one of the great pastoral questions of the day. One thing is clear, however: Our work as servants and sacraments to the modern world will not be entirely effective until we, too, become fluent in the visual language with which the modern world speaks.

3. Modernism's Threat to the Sensual Object

Modern art was born out of a reaction against the excesses of nineteenth-century Romanticism. Its aim has been to pare away everything extraneous to artistic forms in order to reveal what the early modernists called their "internal truths." For many artists this search for ultimate simplicity of expression has represented something of a spiritual journey as well, even if their audiences have failed to recognize it as such. In this vein one thinks immediately of such figures as the American painter Mark Rothko, whose monumental, nonrepresentational images of the 1960s and 1970s document a long, tragic search for the Primordial. "You might as well get something straight," Rothko, a Jew, once instructed an interviewer: "I'm not an abstractionist . . . I'm not interested in the relationship of color or form or anything else. I'm interested in expressing basic human emotions . . . [a]nd the fact that a lot of people break down and cry in front of my pictures shows . . . they are having the same religious experience I had when I painted them."[6]

Modernism's attempt to chasten art of unnecessary sensuality came to its logical conclusion in the 1970s, with the development of so-called "Conceptual Art." By taking the creative act to its ultimate point of reduction, artists of the Conceptual strain eventually eliminated the physical component from their work altogether and turned to projects whose results were mostly theoretical or ephemeral. (In 1976, for example, the sculptor Christo extended his clothesline-like *Running Fence* through twenty-five miles of California countryside, only to have the entire structure of steel and nylon dismantled within weeks of its erection. The point of the project, according to the artist, was not so much to build a fence or any other tangible monument, but to propose an *idea* compelling enough to inspire the collaboration of various workers, landowners, lawyers, bureaucrats, and others.) The art object was now considered incidental; what mattered most was the *concept* that prefigured it. Art itself became more a matter of context than of craft, the creative process grew nearly indistinguishable from philosophy and given to considerable self-reflection.

By the 1970s, modern architecture, too, had reached a point of ultimate formal reduction. Erected in cities throughout the United States were local versions of the sleek, modular buildings popularized by Louis Kahn, Paul Rudolf, Philip Johnson, I. M. Pei, and a cadre of tastemakers at the firm of Skidmore, Owings, and Merrill. The unadorned "glass boxes" of modernism's late phase induced in much of the public what critic Tom Wolfe called "sensory deprivation" and a longing for some vestige of "color and coziness."[7] They were architectural equivalents of the types of minimalist paintings and sculpture then being exhibited at trendy galleries from New York to Los Angeles, as reticent and self-contained as gravestones, which, for modern architecture, they literally were. Architecture students, caught up in the reductivist spirit of the decade, emulated their friends in art school and began speaking with sincerity about "buildings on paper" and even "Conceptual Architecture" that could be erected only in the mind. The ranks of the profession swelled with neophytes who were clumsy with their pencils but eager to argue the relevance of everyone from Karl Marx to Marshall McLuhan.

It is significant that the post-Vatican II reform of Catholic church architecture in the United States commenced in earnest precisely as orthodox modernism was nearing exhaustion. No greater aesthetic sacrifice could

6. Quoted in Suzi Gablik, *Has Modernism Failed?* (London: Thames and Hudson, 1984) 22.
7. *From Bauhaus to Our House* (New York: Farrar, Traus, Giroux, 1981) 4.

American Catholics have been asked to make, in fact, than to abandon the familiar sight of church buildings clad in opulent, historical styles for ones exhibiting the cool reserve of modernism's terminal phase. Catholic sacramentality celebrates ritual sensuality, craftsmanship, and artistic talent—all of which the Church perceives as divine gifts. Prior to the 1970s these gifts were usually embodied in acts of overstatement intended to impress upon even the most boorish pew-sitter the magnificence of God and the hallowedness of God's earthly residence. The local parish church was a showplace of human artistry and a showing-place for the world's Prime Architect, museum and shrine of Tridentine grandeur in one. By the 1970s, however, three things had occurred that would contribute to the wholesale transformation of American Catholic church design: (1) Popular forms of modern design had become fixed parts of the greater visual landscape, manifesting themselves in everything from "Mod" fashions of dress, to the "Avant-Garde" typefaces of corporate letterheads, to the chrome and glass furniture that filled middle-class homes across the country; (2) A generation of liturgical artists and architects had come to maturity that was steeped in Euro-American modernism and excited by its ecclesiastical applications; (3) The episcopal leadership of the Church itself, through a steady stream of postconciliar directives, began to encourage parish communities to employ in their places of worship forms of artistic expression that were authentic to their time and place.

To both priests and laypeople, the combined effect of these forces was overwhelming. Literally within the space of months, the Church ceased making historicization the goal of its architectural projects and turned instead to aggressive *contextualization*. No longer was it sufficient for parishes to erect imitations of architectural monuments from the historic past. The local place of worship now was expected to accommodate a *modern*, streamlined liturgy, freed of "useless repetitions" and adapted to the "needs of our times" (Constitution on the Sacred Liturgy, nos. 34, 62).

From the perspective of aestheticians and art historians, the changes that have transpired in Catholic art and architecture in the decades hence may be interpreted simply as part of a transition from a "romantic" approach to religious-artistic expression to a more "classical" one—one of many such transitions that together comprise the linear evolution of Western art.[8] There has been nothing simple about the reforms of Vatican II for the faithful, however, who, to apply again the words of Tom Wolfe, are still adjusting to "the light-

8. Western art history is said to manifest alternate phases of classicism and romanticism. During the former, the dominant artistic impulse is toward rationality, simplicity, understatement, and so forth. Modernism emerged during one such phase. The austerity we detect in works of modern painting, sculpture, and architecture is a classical trait and attributable to the generally conservative cultural mood of our time.

ness & brightness & cleanness & bareness & spareness"[9] they equate with modern church design.

Conclusions

In this essay I have argued that the reason Catholics in the United States fail to accept modern design as a component of their liturgical lives is that they regard it as a threat to time-honored traditions, to communal life, and to ritual sensuality. I believe, however, that what really terrifies American Catholics is the extent to which we detect our own reflection in modernism's cold, polished surfaces. We are "*crypto*-modernists," all of us, and it makes us squirm.

The Catholics who retain my consulting services, for example, dream of owning the newest homes in the newest, suburban housing developments. They wear the latest fashions, speak knowingly about the latest books and films, the latest talkshow scandals. They have mastered New Age philosophy and the politics of the New World Order. Copies of the New Catechism decorate their coffee tables. Their kids play with the hottest video games, pierce and shave and tattoo their body parts in the most novel ways, drop the trendiest slang at the dinner table. They pay good money to update their kitchens, perk up their bathrooms, and side their homes in vinyl. Shiny, new vans, boats, and campers fill their driveways. In short, their lives are open to the same kind of novelty that has been modernism's chief obsession from the beginning. Like loyal modernists, too, they relish their independence—freedom from friends, neighbors, extended families—and prefer their sense experiences in manageable doses. The lives of American Catholics are unavoidably *modern*, and they turn to religion and art to keep themselves connected to the past.

There is, I think, a strong relationship between the shared need to treat our brand-new, suburban split-levels to every sort of Shaker or Victorian or Neo-Georgian nicknack available, scenting the whole of them with batches of exotic-smelling potpourri, and our need as modern American Catholics to fill our Sabbath settings with the "bells and smells" and artifacts of a bygone age. Somewhere along the way we developed the idea that neither religion nor art should question the status quo, but that their primary function is to restate in the most accessible ways what is already known and accepted. What we seek in art, then, is actually sedation; what we desire from religion are pleasant ritual exercises. We cannot allow either to change too much, or our blissful equilibrium would be undone. (The phenomenon shows up elsewhere. Music directors of the nation's symphony orchestras regularly complain that their paying audiences will not

9. *From Bauhaus to Our House*, 4.

tolerate the performance of contemporary music of any kind. Consequently, the typical orchestra concert today is an elaborate exercise in musical conservancy in which performers dutifully replicate only "old chestnuts.")

"We know what we like," Catholic building committees claim as they go about assembling their liturgical environments—to which pastors and ordinaries, if they truly wish to teach, should reply: "You *like* what you *know*, and what you know about sacred worship and design may be limited." Though we claim universality at every chance, our tastes are strictly parochial. With a wave of the hand we dismiss any art form that strikes us as foreign or more intellectually demanding than the average TV commercial. The arrogance is appalling.

Short of offering their parishioners formal training in modern aesthetics, there is little that pastors can do to expand the visual diet of a parish community. In the foreseeable future, in fact, our churches will likely continue to operate on two cultural levels—one "high," one "low." The former, which at times in ecclesiastical history was open mainly to the clergy, is comprised of those faithful who, for whatever reason, have had access to a wide range of artistic experiences and consider the fine arts, literature, music, dance, and theater to be essential parts of daily life. The latter involves those believers for whom art of any kind is of little consequence. (Curiously, the Catholics who complain the loudest about changes in the Church's worship and art are those who seem to have the least knowledge of liturgical and artistic tradition.)

What concrete steps can pastors take to help believers in both cultural spheres to appreciate modern liturgical design? Here are several:

- Through formal or informal means, learn more for yourself about the place that modernism holds in the long history of Western art. Primers on the subject abound, and one might even begin with a specialized text, like Jaroslav Pelikan's *Jesus Through the Centuries* (New Haven: Yale, 1985), which nicely outlines the historical evolution of Christian art and symbolism.

- Slowly and selectively begin to introduce into your parish's ritual setting good examples of modern design. A set of original liturgical vessels, a good-quality vestment, a handsome processional cross in the modern style, etc., can help to link modernism to sacred activity in the minds of parishioners. (Imitate the Holy Father in this. In his public appearances, John Paul II carries a beautiful, modern crosier, which, when juxtaposed to his traditional vesture, celebrates the continuity of Christian art.)

- Designate a place in your parish's worship building apart from the liturgical center where works of art can be exhibited. Let modern examples occupy this space from time to time, along with some written explanation of the artists' intentions.

- Incorporate elements of modern design into the parish's printed materials (bulletins, liturgical programs, music sheets, etc.). Images have a way of subliminally imprinting themselves on the mind. If modern images appear routinely in parishioners' hands, they may eventually become part of the collection of images they carry in their heads.

If, in the words of Vatican II, modern art is to "add its own voice to that wonderful chorus of praise sung by the great masters of past ages of Catholic faith" (Constitution on the Sacred Liturgy, no. 123), pastors and ordinaries must first invite it to do so. Motivating this invitation must be a profound respect for the Church's artistic patrimony and, at the same time, a conviction that the Holy Spirit is still capable of inspiring greatness in today's image-makers and builders. Ours is indeed a long and venerable tradition of artistic production, to which we should add with pride and confidence the visual gestures of praise and praycr of the generations that currently inhabit the planet.

PART TWO

6

WORSHIPING IN "NOPLACE": CASUAL OBSERVATIONS ON AMERICAN CATHOLIC LITURGY IN THE SECOND MACHINE AGE

I anticipate the scowls at the outset of every academic semester after informing male students in my university-level art history courses that they are forbidden to wear hats of any kind in the classroom. The amazed and angry faces return on those occasions when I lead students, nearly all of whom claim religious upbringing, through the interiors of various church buildings and must likewise remind men to bare their heads in deference to their surroundings.

Getting today's male undergraduates to part with their beloved headwear is virtually impossible, of course. As any observer of American youth culture knows, hats, especially in the form of baseball and golf caps, have become essential features of self-identity to males age fifteen to thirty-five. Fixed to the head at every conceivable angle, they are as important to the typical pop fashion statement as multiple earrings, tattoos, and hundred-dollar gym shoes. One sees them being worn at all times and everywhere—in libraries, banks, and corporate offices, in the finest restaurants, in concert halls and theaters, funeral parlors and hospital corridors—all without the least measure of concern for public decorum.

The very idea, in fact, that there might continue to exist rules of public order strikes many as laughable today. "You can't enforce a universal dress code, for God's sake," a colleague of mine argues. Perhaps not. Yet there was a time, not long ago, when it seemed that most of us knew instinctively or by rearing the difference between appropriate behavior and that which might appear juvenile, wrong-headed, or just plain offensive. No matter how one acted or dressed behind closed doors, under public scrutiny one conformed to the mores of the group. One saw oneself, in fact, as *part* of a group and understood that rules of civility—however arbitrary or artificial—were necessary if we all hoped to occupy the public square together in peace.

Such is not the case today, a fact made plain daily in my classroom. The so-called "student body" I encounter there is really little more than an amorphous crowd of automatons whose random collisions with each other produce considerable friction but scarcely any warmth or light. They share no more concern for maintaining a "community of learners" than they do for anything else that might require prolonged commitment to each other. Their aim is never to be pinned down, never to be tethered to persons or politics or high-minded causes, but to move fluidly from one private experience to another, like channel surfers busily fingering the controls of their TV remotes.

What has all of this to do with the way American Catholics worship? Plenty, I would suggest, if the Church continues to uphold the importance of prayer that is communal and of places so charged with beauty and meaning that they assume a sacramental character. What one detects in the nation's youth is only the most overt expression of the kind of self-absorption that pervades the populace as a whole, even within such ostensibly corporate entities as the Church. It is not hard, for example, to find Catholic households in the United States full of members who orbit each other at a distance, frenetically, without the simplest of domestic rituals to bind them. Shared meals are something that even Catholic families now associate only with the nostalgia of Norman Rockwell paintings or reruns of "The Waltons." And shared prayer? If the emptiness of church pews is any indication, most in the fold abandon this, too, soon after the fragrance of chrism departs them.

It does not help that Catholics in the United States find themselves immersed in a wider culture that seems increasingly to militate against any form of genuine communion between individuals, the kind once fostered by extended families, ethnic enclaves, and old-fashioned neighborhoods. Neither is it helpful that a number of sociotechnological forces have conjoined to diminish peoples' sense of place and, in turn, of place-related behavior. Concerning the latter, author James Howard Kunstler[1] suggests that Americans have so degraded their physical environment, so trivialized the design of the work-

1. *The Geography of Nowhere* (New York: Simon and Schuster, 1993).

place and home, so homogenized the landscape with look-alike edifices as to have literally lost their location in the world. In a topography lacerated by superhighways and littered with "cartoon buildings and commercial images," one site becomes indistinguishable from another, one site-specific experience no more significant than the next. The result is one great, characterless "Nowhere," as arid as the American soul. "Such an arrangement," Kunstler concludes, "has certainly done away with sacred places, places of public assembly and places of casual repose."[2] Kunstler is not alone in his criticism of the country's nomadic impulse, its addiction to automobility and related technologies that free a restless people from situating itself firmly in space and time. Syndicated columnist Bob Greene has lamented recently the loss of "the purely local" and defines the national credo as: "You [don't] have to be anywhere."[3] Similarly, Paul Goldberger of the *New York Times* notes with caution the advent of a boundless, electronic "Nowhere Land" offering vast numbers of computer-users the illusion of communal experience. "We hear continually about cyberspace as a place of connections made between people who would not have come together before," Goldberger observes, "[b]ut every one of them has connected by being alone, in front of a computer screen."[4] (For subscribers to the Internet, spatial proximity between living, breathing creatures is replaced by electronic proximity, which, sadly enough, explains the system's immense popularity.) Each of these writers is merely echoing the work of Jane Jacobs, who was one of the first analysts of built culture to realize that changes in the American lifestyle were blurring geographic identities and helping to make "every place . . . more like every other place, all adding up to Noplace." "Today," Jacobs stated over forty years ago, in her prophetic text, *The Death and Life of Great American Cities*, "everyone who loves cities is disturbed by automobiles":

> Traffic arteries, along with parking lots, gas stations and drive-ins, are power-full and insistent instruments of city destruction. To accommodate them, city streets are broken down into loose sprawls, incoherent and vacuous for anyone afoot. Downtowns and other neighborhoods that are marvels of close-grained intricacy and compact mutual support are casually disemboweled. Landmarks are crumbled or are so sundered from their contexts in city life as to become irrelevant trivialities. . . . It is questionable how much of the destruction . . . is really a response to transportation and traffic needs, and how much is owing to sheer disrespect for other city needs, uses and functions.[5]

2. *The Geography of Nowhere*, 119.
3. "Reality . . . TV . . . Reality . . . TV," *Erie Daily Times* (January 10, 1994) 5.
4. "Cyberspace Trips to Nowhere Land," *New York Times* (October 5, 1995) B1.
5. *The Death and Life of Great American Cities* (New York: Vintage 1961) 338–39.

While such trends will likely not cause the Church to devise a variety of "McEucharists," "cyberliturgies" or sacraments conferred by fiber-optic impulse, the prevailing rage in the United States to reduce all experience to the glow of a computer screen or windshield-framed abstractions has already begun to affect in substantial ways Catholics' attitudes toward ritual prayer. Of concern to everyone from pastors to liturgists to designers of sacred spaces, for example, is the growing indifference displayed by the faithful toward the physical setting of worship. As transient residents of the landscape of sameness—all tract housing, convenience stores, and Taco Bells—American Catholics (like the rest of their compatriots) have been anesthetized to the effects of real architecture, the kind that speaks through historical allusion or complex relationships of space and form. Gone are the great public works of the past, big, chunky buildings dressed in formal attire that taught us as much about moving and acting with elegant deliberateness as a new suit of clothes. Today, instead, we envelop ourselves in a confection of drywall and suspended ceilings handily concealed beneath every sort of artificial material—a pasteboard habitat that invites no more emotional commitment from us than the average motel room. The casualness with which American Catholics treat sacred places, then, is simply an extension of the blasé attitude we bring to every other corner of our built environment. It is a response elicited to a certain extent by the visual landscape itself, which we curse for its blandness even while racing off to the opening of another megamall.

Fifty years ago, perhaps, it was easier for American Catholics to escape the banality of the secular realm for places that seemed otherworldly. One had only to pass beyond the threshold of any parish church building to enter a repository of familiar anachronisms carefully preserved from the twin threats of modernist thought and art. It made little difference to the laity that the role offered them in the Church's official rites was virtually nonexistent. They loved their places of worship, mortgaged their futures to erect them, and took considerable pride in the lavish stage-settings for the Tridentine Mass that their sacrificial dollars could pay for. To the Catholic imagination, space itself was something "heterogeneous," "broken" or "interrupted," to borrow from Mircea Eliade's[6] famous treatment of the matter. It consisted of dry, desert-like places through which believers moved, seemingly untouched by divine grace, and those spaces literally bathed in sanctity. (Is it not partly by means of a sprinkling rite that the Church continues to confer sacred status upon its liturgical settings?) Distinguishing the two was easy. Sacred spaces, like those

6. *The Sacred and the Profane*, William A. Trusk, trans. (New York: Harcourt, Brace, Jovanovich 1959) 20.

contained in our churches, looked, smelled, and felt as if they had been around for*ever*; the dust collected in them was traceable to Eden or Calvary or ancient Rome. Secular spaces, on the other hand, lacked the aura of antiquity and thus seemed unlikely dwelling places for a God as old as ours. The difference was illusory, of course, an effect achieved by filling our churches with catalog reproductions of Old World splendor while we cast the rest of our surroundings in the very latest visual fashions. It did not jibe well with our belief in the sanctity of all creation, either, or in a flesh-and-blood Messiah who left the whole world shimmering by his earthly presence. Nevertheless, it was precisely the formality of Catholic worship and its architectural environment in those days prior to Vatican II that helped Catholics feel that they were involved in something special and, indeed, salvific. High Mass was high art, at least to untrained eyes, and the more it elevated human words and actions beyond the realm of the commonplace, the better.

While it has become popular to blame the reforms of Vatican II for the perceived deterioration of Catholic worship and art, I am convinced that the crisis of liturgical style currently facing American Catholics would have arisen had the Council never been convoked in the first place. We function in a country preoccupied with leisurely play and entertainment, both of which find visual expression in gestures of *in*formality. "Life is short. Play hard," the advertising campaigns for Reebok, Inc., proclaim, as they help turn running shoes and tailored sweatsuits into the national uniform. (If we can't exactly perform as our celebrity athletes do, the message seems to be, at least we can all *look* like them.)

It comes as no surprise that designer Ralph Lauren should recently introduce a line of decorative paints whose colors include "Stadium Red," "Lap Pool Blue," "Hockey Puck," and "Gymnast." Lauren, who has amassed a fortune selling Americans on the idea of casual chic, knows that the symbolism of sport affiliation now supersedes that of class, politics—even religion. So, too, do the people behind the "Calvin Kline Sport" label or the chummy, pseudo-cosmopolitan "United Colors of Benetton." One has only to survey any weekend Mass crowd in an American Catholic parish to realize the extent to which these tastemakers have democratized loose-fitting, informal dress more suitable for the locker room than for the sanctuary. And the resultant clash of iconographies is staggering: The Church continues to vest its clergy in the style of Imperial Rome while the pews teem with flashy sports insignias and corporate logos of every sort. Communion processions have become one extended advertisement for the nation's fashion industry, more related to hype than to hope.

Recently, on the country's highest holy day, Super Bowl Sunday, I was required to speak from the pulpit during Mass at a parish where everyone but the presider was dressed in the colors of the local favorites. Even the altar servers wore the obligatory hues beneath their albs and proudly displayed them with each genuflection. Strangely, it was the *priest's* attire that seemed out of place, along with lofty words and music whose importance was eclipsed by the spirit of THE GAME. On another occasion I was met at the door of a parish church by a priest wearing the most resplendent Eastertide garments and, standing immediately beside him, by a boy in a "Beavis and Butt-Head" T-shirt. The juxtaposition of sacred and profane, the virtual *merging* of the two, was astounding, and I was left to consider how thorough has been the hybridization of American and Catholic cultures. In the space of, say, two generations, Catholics in the United States have exchanged the "cap-and-lunch-pail" identity of their immigrant past for the requisite emblems of middle-class comfort. (Curiously, the caps have remained intact!) If we nowadays "dress down" for the Sabbath, it is because most of us have spent the balance of the workweek in starchy business clothes—the opposite of our grandparents, who "dressed up" for church services as respite from a week's worth of aprons and overalls. (An exception exists in African-American and Hispanic parishes, where the habit of dressing up for church generally persists.)

The Church's accumulation of material wealth has not brought with it a corresponding increase in wisdom or grace, however, and while our lives may be considerably *easier* than those of our predecessors, one senses that they are touched less often by the simple poetry of touch, taste, sight, and sound. One also wonders whether there is not something about the American temperament and a national ethos favoring self-reliance that frustrates our attempts to pray in ways that are truly liturgical. Worshiping as a unified, ecclesial body challenges us to entrust ourselves to God and each other, as any occasion of sacramental love does. It asks that we rub shoulders with perfect strangers so as to recognize in them Christ's own redemptive presence.

Unfortunately, three decades after being reminded by Vatican II that "[l]iturgical services are not private functions but celebrations belonging to the [entire] church, which is the 'sacrament of unity'. . ." (Constitution on the Sacred Liturgy, no. 26), the average American Catholic worshiper remains disinclined to contribute his or her voice to the Church's common prayer. Much of the blame for this condition lies squarely with the American episcopate, which has yet to formulate a systematic plan for teaching the faithful how to worship as the conciliar documents would have them (strange for an administrative body so fond of the title "magisterial"). Diocesan liturgy offices are chronically understaffed and thus cannot conduct within their respective territories the kind of comprehensive instruction of adults that is needed.

As I see it, however, the greatest impediment to American Catholic liturgical renewal lies not within the walls of the Church but outside them, where believers are now treated to an array of mechanical spectacles more alluring than anything the Church has to offer in its scared rites. Forget about real words, real gestures, real food, Real Presence—all of which pale in comparison with the packaged thrills of this new machine age. What we want are lives played out like interactive videos, neat and antiseptic, with only the simulation of human relationships to complicate them. We crave our privacy, our independence, and, at least for the present fashion moment, the right to wear our ball caps wherever we damned well please.

7

IMAGES
BY WHICH WE LIVE AND BUILD

Catholicism is a faith guided by sacramental instinct. It embraces the divine not as intellectual proposition but as flesh and blood. It is a faith born of a Mediterranean culture, one that "speaks with its hands." Yet, for all the richness of experience that sacramentality is said to impart to Catholic life, it is rare that we detect in our local church buildings any real appreciation for the workings of ritual action, for symbol, for poetry and art—those things which nourish the soul, keep the heart supple, and point us beyond ourselves. We confess belief in the consecrative power of baptism, yet only reluctantly do we regard ourselves sources of holiness for the world. We claim inheritance of an ancient tradition of belief, yet ours is a Church largely ignorant of its past, struggling to be prophetic to present generations. We are, it seems, a people whose great aspirations are forever weighed down by stubborn attachment to the prosaic, and if sin does not weaken the authority of our message, mediocrity no doubt will.

These contradictions in Catholic behavior come to light whenever a parish gathers to discuss the environment for worship, because the construction or renovation of a church obliges a community to scrutinize its liturgical habits and the beliefs that lie behind them. All too often, unfortunately, what emerges from such self-examination are notions of prayer that are at odds with the Church's stated understanding of liturgy. Accordingly, building committee members will insist that the only appropriate setting for Catholic worship is an immense and lavishly appointed space, somehow medieval in complexion, with stained-glass windows, two clearly distinguishable precincts for the respective actions of clergy and laity, and a tabernacle of such size and prominence as to be visible from the remotest corner. To the popular imagination the Catholic church building remains a site of divine residence wherein the sacred and the beautiful are together preserved from despoilment. We reverence our buildings as temples, still, or shrines for the Blessed Sacrament, though the vision of sacred architecture proposed by the Church's official legislation is a decidedly different one.

To be sure, our mental images of the American Catholic place of worship are partly a reflection of the architectural record itself, which, prior to Vatican II, was dominated by structures imitative of the large scale and opulence of European models. Equally influential as shapers of the Catholic architectural imagination, however, are the printed images of sacred buildings that have long filled the pages of the Church's various catechetical publications. It is as if believers share a common paradigm of design, fairly strict in its definition, formed by the mental fusing of two distinct types of experience: (1) that derived from encounters with actual sacred places, and (2) that linked to pictorial representations of sacred places—the kind impressed upon the mind in childhood, perhaps, and never revised or refined with maturity. To appreciate the attitudes that Catholics bring to their architectural projects, then, we must become as familiar with a heritage of buildings rendered on paper as with one erected in stone.

Pictorial Representations of Catholic Architecture

Pictorial representations of American Catholic church buildings published since, say, World War II provide valuable traces of how the Church has visualized its liturgical accommodations for the purpose of catechesis. An illustration accompanying a definition of the word "church" from the 1948 *Catholic Picture Dictionary* (Catholic Manufacturing Company), for example, essentially catalogs the requisite parts of the building designed to serve the Tridentine Rite Mass (fig. 26). Here, image and text make clear that a church is a building detached from its secular surroundings and reserved for both devotional and liturgical prayer, the foci of which stand in close proximity within an expansive tableau of rarefied objects. Though the imaginary building exhibits nave and apse spaces in a familiar, basilican arrangement, its distinctly "ecclesiastical" appearance owes more to recurring references to the Gothic building style, such as the great, pointed arches framing the sanctuary and ancillary chapels and the running arcade that marks the apsidal niche.

The building shows no signs of human occupancy yet seems perfect and complete, even in its emptiness, like the perfectly ordered but vacant interiors displayed in popular "home and garden" magazines. This is, after all, an illustration of the dwelling place of God as defined in purely architectural terms.

The image of the church building as depository of the sacred is presented similarly in *These Are Our Neighbors* (Ginn and Company), a primary grade reader that was popular in Catholic schools throughout the 1940s and 1950s. In one of the book's stories, the main characters, two school children named Mark and Joan, visit for the first time the rural church where their grandparents worship. Initially the children are struck by the building's modest size: "Is that a church?" Mark asks, voicing common

CHURCH (cherch)
A building set apart for the public worship of Almighty God, and designed to be used only for this purpose.

Fig. 26—Illustration accompanying the word "church" from *Catholic Picture Dictionary*.

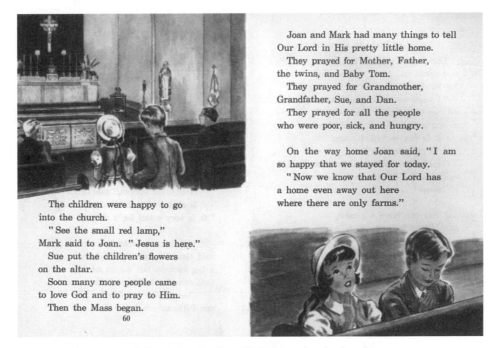

The children were happy to go into the church.
"See the small red lamp," Mark said to Joan. "Jesus is here."
Sue put the children's flowers on the altar.
Soon many more people came to love God and to pray to Him.
Then the Mass began.
60

Joan and Mark had many things to tell Our Lord in His pretty little home.
They prayed for Mother, Father, the twins, and Baby Tom.
They prayed for Grandmother, Grandfather, Sue, and Dan.
They prayed for all the people who were poor, sick, and hungry.

On the way home Joan said, "I am so happy that we stayed for today.
"Now we know that Our Lord has a home even away out here where there are only farms."

Fig. 27a & b—Images of church interior from Catholic grade school reader.

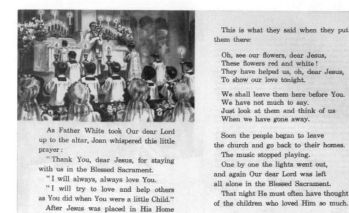

As Father White took Our dear Lord up to the altar, Joan whispered this little prayer:

" Thank You, dear Jesus, for staying with us in the Blessed Sacrament.

" I will always, always love You.

" I will try to love and help others as You did when You were a little Child."

After Jesus was placed in His Home on the altar, the little girls went up and left their beautiful flowers before the Blessed Sacrament.

252

This is what they said when they put them there:

Oh, see our flowers, dear Jesus,
These flowers red and white !
They have helped us, oh, dear Jesus,
To show our love tonight.

We shall leave them here before You.
We have not much to say.
Just look at them and think of us
When we have gone away.

Soon the people began to leave the church and go back to their homes. The music stopped playing. One by one the lights went out, and again Our dear Lord was left all alone in the Blessed Sacrament.

That night He must often have thought of the children who loved Him so much.

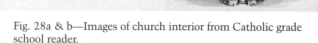

Fig. 28a & b—Images of church interior from Catholic grade school reader.

assumptions. "It is very small for a church." Nevertheless, an accompanying illustration assures readers that the structure in question lacks none of the interior fixtures peculiar to the Catholic place of prayer (figs. 27a and b; see page 89). Indeed, the scene is one of canonical propriety in which everything from tabernacle to papal flag has been assigned a station of relative importance in a strictly compartmentalized corridor of sanctity. "See the small red lamp," Mark announces with relief. "Jesus is here." The image affirms the long-standing Catholic belief that space is not homogeneous, that there exists a hierarchy of places on the earthly plane, and, as the characters conclude, that "Our Lord has a home even . . . where there are only farms."

Another story from the same source describes the characters' participation in a solemn rite of eucharistic benediction. Two illustrations on adjacent pages complement this story, the first of which conveys the visual splendor of the event as its principal parts unfold within an incense-filled sanctuary (fig. 28a). At the heart of the scene a priest holds aloft an elaborate monstrance, his figure surrounded by the forms of attendant ministers, altar boys, and ceremonial décor. The exclusively male goings-on of the sanctuary are watched from a distance by a row of veiled girls, one of whom is Joan, whose attention, we are told, comes to rest on a beautifully vested tabernacle depicted in isolation by the story's second illustration (fig. 28b). This is Jesus' "Home on the altar," the text informs us, as literal a place of residence as the home of any Catholic boy or girl. In this vessel the sacramental Christ is enshrined as a kind of parochial resident of honor, and it is in the familiar setting of their parish churches that readers can gain privileged access to him.

It should be noted that such images of the style and environment of Catholic worship are not exclusive to publications for children. When, for example, the National Catholic Welfare Conference (forerunner of the United States Catholic Conference) published its English translations of Pius XII's famous *Mediator Dei* (1947) and, a decade later, the Sacred Congregation of Rites' *Musica Sacra et Sacra Liturgia* (1958), the documents carried identical cover illustrations depicting the interior of a large Gothic church filled with worshipers (fig. 29). Most intriguing about this example is the disparity in size between that portion of the image devoted to aspects of sacred environment and that which represents the sacred assembly. The latter constitutes only a fraction of the compositional scheme, and the figures of worshipers it offers are diminutive and faceless. They are legible only as elements in a generalized mass at the image's base, visual footnotes to a statement that, again, is primarily about architecture. In this instance the church building is celebrated less as a bearer of liturgical action than as a splendid object, vast in its vertical dimension, lavish in its detailing, and illuminated by shafts of "divine light."

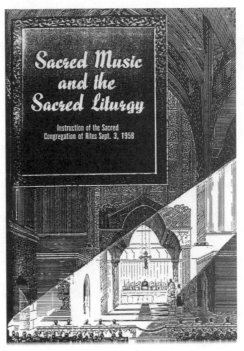

Fig. 29—Cover illustration from *Musica Sacra et Sacra Liturgia*.

Not surprising is the frequency with which Gothic forms appear in representations of Catholic architecture, for Gothicism continues to hold an elevated place in the Church's historical memory. Today, in fact, the style enjoys almost iconic status among the faithful, and its quintessential element, the pointed arch, is part of a stylistic shorthand employed as readily by illustrators as by architects to evoke religious associations in their

Keep the Lord's Day Holy.

Fig. 30—Image of church façade from *St. Joseph Baltimore Cathechism*.

Fig. 31—Illustration from *We Go to Mass.*

works. The reduction of so complex a design style as the Gothic to a single, representative motif is demonstrated in an illustration from the 1962 edition of the *St. Joseph Baltimore Catechism* (Catholic Book Publishing Company) that shows members of a Catholic family proceeding toward the entrance of a church on their way to Mass (fig. 30; see page 91). The implied Gothic styling of the building's entrance portal and interior vaulting functions emblematically to establish the ecclesiastical nature of an otherwise nondescript architectural form, and the scene's message is immediate: Catholics properly worship in Gothic buildings, even in the last half of the twentieth century. So enduring is this pictorial theme that it appears in virtually the same form a quarter-century later on the cover of *We Go to Mass*, a publication of Regina Press (Malhame and Company; fig. 31). Comparison of these two examples suggests that while the attire worn by Catholics to worship may change with time and even grow more casual, the attire of our buildings retains its formality and historical references. In fact, a survey of imagery from the majority of contemporary catechetical sources leads one to conclude that Catholic architecture is inherently anachronistic and that the Church knows of no other style in which to build than the Gothic (see figs. 32 & 33 on page 93; fig. 34 on page 94). Perhaps it is the sheer pervasiveness of this Gothic emblem that inclines even Catholic children from parishes with decidedly *non*-Gothic buildings to perceive their places of worship as spiky, Gothic rocket ships pointed toward a celestial canopy (fig. 35; see page 95).

Conclusions

While it may be argued that images like the ones included in this study are simply too juvenile or innocuous to have much bearing on the Church's architectural practices, persons working closely with parish building committees will recognize their connection to the sentiments often brought to the planning and design table. The sad truth is that Catholics typically assume their work as church-builders equipped with little more than the memorized fragments of their earliest religious instruction. To speak of worshipers "shaping the liturgical environment" or conferring upon it the sanctity of their own baptismal identity is thus to baffle many of the faithful, who yet conceive of their buildings as intrinsically sacred and autonomous entities capable of standing apart from the rites they house.

To remedy this situation, parishes must set about reeducating themselves, a task that will necessarily involve reappraisal of the images by which they live and build. Reeducation might begin with careful examination of the New Testament, whose books caution Christians repeatedly against ascribing too great a sacrality to the buildings we erect or presuming that through them we

I am glad when I go to God's house.
Based on Psalm 122:1

Fig. 32.—Promotional illustration for *Christ Our Life* catechetical series.

might somehow contain or confine the presence of Almighty God. On this point the epistles of Saints Peter and Paul, especially, are emphatic: God is not to be found at the periphery of human experience, lodged in tent or tabernacle, but dwells at the heart of an ecclesial body made sacred in its humanity and dispersed beyond the confines of any earthly sanctuary. It is from the table, not

the temple, that we Christians draw our strength, where Christ's glory is laid bare, savored and consumed by people hungry for salvation. For *this* action we build, apart from which even our grandest buildings seem absent of meaning.

Equally essential to parishes are the cotents of the major liturgical

14 *Our Christian community celebrates Jesus' presence.*

We come together as a community
in church or at home.
We do this to celebrate the Lord's presence.
We praise and thank God our Father,
with words and gesture,
with song and silent prayer.
We eat a special meal together.
We call this the Eucharist.

Jesus says, "Where two or three are gathered
in my name, there am I in their midst."
Matthew 18:20

Fig. 33—Illustration from *The Christian Community*, by Carl Pfeifer and Janaan Manternach.

Lesson 9
We Worship God

We Share

Do you go to church on Saturday nights or Sundays?

Why do we go to church?

We Listen

Jesus' family, the Church, worships the Father together. Worship is very special. It is the way we show God that we know we need him. It is the way we show God our love. It is the way we thank him.

God our Father is so great and so wonderful! We want to praise him.

God has given us many gifts! We want to say "Thank you."

God is so patient with us. We want to tell him we are sorry for doing wrong things, for hurting others and for not loving enough.

God is so loving! We can pray for what we need or want.

When we worship, we do not just talk. We also listen. God speaks to us through his Word in the Bible.

> **Word Box**
> worship

Fig. 34—Illustration from *Jesus Teaches Us*.

documents of our day, which uphold the image of the worshiping assembly as origin and shaper of all good church design. In their dealings with architects and related design professionals, parish groups must be cognizant of recent legislation and intent upon devising places for ritual that truly embody unity, holiness, and the participatory character of the Church at prayer. Parishes that give more than a superficial reading to this legislation will likely devote greater attention to the functional capabilities of their proposed church buildings than to such secondary matters as style and decorative treatment.

Parishes must also become acquainted with the long history of Christian worship and its setting, for historical acknowledge at once tempers our delight in novelty and reveals the true life-span of conventions popularly revered as "traditional." History reminds us of the inescapable temporality of our work as builders, its connection to time and place and culture, and that the first condition of all liturgical art is to make the sacred meaningful to its beholders. "God does not need liturgy," the Bishops' Committee on the Liturgy have reminded us, "people do; and people have only their own art and styles of expression with which to celebrate" (*Environment and Art in Catholic Worship*, no. 4). We who presume to communicate with God and each other by sacramental-artistic means do so only to the degree that we comprehend the media of our communication. Thus the buildings we erect for liturgical purposes must announce the reality of redemption in ways that are authentic to our age, or they may be dismissed as utterly irrelevant.

In the end, however, no amount of scriptural or legislative or historical information will guarantee the success of a parish's labor if it is not absolutely grounded in prayer. Prayer must be both the *reason* we build or renovate churches and the *means* by which we discern Christ's guidance in our work. Prayer mitigates the ill-effects of rumor, egoism, and contention which often frustrate even the best building projects. And it may be only through prayer that parishes will find the courage to reform the conceptual imagery that inspires both the faith and the actions of their members.

Fig. 35—Child's drawing of a church.

8

THE QUEST FOR
"NOBLE SIMPLICITY"[1]

Among the greatest challenges to designers of contemporary Catholic architecture is the Church's recommendation that their works embody a "noble
simplicity" (*General Instruction on the Roman Missal*, no. 279). Official
liturgical directives make clear that a building for sacred worship must promote the common experience of its users and focus their attention on specific
poles of ritual action. Accordingly, designers are instructed to refrain from the
inflated scale and excessive ornamentation characteristic of Catholic architecture erected prior to the council, which, reformers argue, tended to call attention only to themselves. Instead they are encouraged to devise places for
prayer of such modesty that their forms virtually recede from view when
pressed into service by an assembly of worshipers. Such, the Church advises,
is the necessary task of artists involved in liturgical expression, for the overt
beauty of their works must never obscure that more fundamental Mystery
that lies beyond mere surface allure. The revised place of Catholic liturgy
must stand window-like and iconic—a thing not so much to be looked at as to
be looked *through* by believers anxious to glimpse the Divine.

1. This essay is based on a paper presented at "Making Sacred Places," the Sixth International and Inter-
disciplinary Conference on Built Form and Culture Research, hosted in 1997 by the University of Cincinnati
College of Design, Architecture, Art and Planning, Hebrew Union College and Old Saint George Church of
Cincinnati. I wish to thank Professor John Hancock of the University of Cincinnati for his preliminary review
of this work.

In this essay I wish to explain why "noble simplicity" has proven to be such an elusive goal to persons involved in the reform of Catholic architecture in the United States and why there persists today such disparity between the Church's stated intentions and the design tendencies of the average American Catholic parish. The essay will attempt to identify the sources of popular Catholic tastes and suggest why the lay population generally has been slow to embrace the new liturgical aesthetic formulated by promoters of change. The study will conclude with analyses of select examples of recent church design that reflect some of the ways in which "noble simplicity" is now incorporated into American Catholic architecture.

The Church's Teachings on "Noble Simplicity"

The Church's teachings on "noble simplicity" as a condition of contemporary worship space were made clear at the outset of Vatican II in the Constitution on the Sacred Liturgy. Article 34 of the constitution employed the phrase explicitly and noted that Catholic worship services themselves should be "short, clear and unencumbered by useless repetitions." These general prescriptions were in turn applied to the physical setting for liturgy in a section of the constitution that encouraged overseers of sacred properties to maintain "noble beauty rather then mere sumptuous display" (ch. 7, no. 124). In a statement that carried important implications for the decorative treatment of church buildings and the spatial arrangement of their devotional contents, the constitution offered the following instructions:

> The practice of placing sacred images in churches so that they may be venerated by the faithful is to be maintained. Nevertheless, there is to be restraint regarding their number and prominence so that they do not create confusion among the Christian people or foster religious practices of doubtful orthodoxy (no. 126).

The premise underlying each of these conciliar statements is that the Catholic place of worship, which previously served the needs of passive lay worshipers consumed in private, devotional prayer, should be remade into an environment supportive of truly corporate action. Architecture fulfills its liturgical role, the bishops of Vatican II declared, not by offering worshipers isolated and randomly scattered stimuli for personal meditation, but by clarifying the view of an assembly actively involved in the highest expression of ecclesial unity. Achieving the latter, the bishops acknowledged, might require the suppression of elements extraneous to the central acts of liturgical prayer or the outright removal from sacred places of furnishings judged to be of inferior artistic quality (Constitution on the Sacred Liturgy, no. 12).

The virtues of clarity, understatement, and right ordering in sacred design were restated in the *General Instruction on the Roman Missal* promulgated in 1969. "In keeping with the [C]hurch's very ancient tradition," the *General Instruction* explains, "it is lawful to set up in places of worship images of Christ, Mary and the saints for veneration by the faithful." "Nevertheless," reads the proviso that follows, "there is need both to limit their number and to situate them in such a way that they do not distract the people's attention from the celebration":

> There is to be only one image of any one saint. In general, the devotion of the entire community is to be the criterion regarding images in the adornment and arrangement of a church (no. 278).

Like the Constitution on the Sacred Liturgy, the *General Instruction* is explicit in its endorsement of architectural forms that are at once noble and simple. In a section entitled "The General Plan of the Church," the *General Instruction* notes that the style and decoration of a church building should be free of "ostentation" but convey instead both "genuineness" and "the dignity of the place of worship" (no. 312). "Even in minor matters," the *Instruction* recommends, "every effort should be made to respect the canons of art and to combine cleanliness and noble simplicity" (no. 312).

"Art chosen for the place of worship," *Built of Living Stones* warns parishes in the United States, "is not simply something pretty or well made. . . . Nor is the place of worship a museum to house masterpieces or artistic models" (no. 143). Quality resides instead, the instruction argues, in the "honesty and genuineness" (no. 146) of a sacred building's materials; and, though Catholic architectural tradition has certainly produced "sublime places of . . . awe-inspiring beauty," it has likewise found value in "humble places of worship that, in their simplicity, inspire a sense of the sacred" (no. 141).

The Coincidence of Catholic Architectural Reform and the Flourishing of High Modernism

In a noteworthy historical coincidence, Catholic architectural reform commenced just as modernism in the creative arts was reaching its terminal, most aggressively reductivist phase. To many Catholics, the simultaneous appearance after Vatican II of novel modes of worship and new, overtly *modern* means of visual expression represented the undoing of much that was considered timeless, immutable, and true. Modernism came late to the Church at large, having been suppressed for a century or so by the prevailing impulse among Catholics to preserve sacred art from the swiftly changing fashions and aesthetic trends that seemed to define modernity itself. When

Fig. 36a—Traditional Catholic church interior before Vatican II.

the style finally arrived, full-blown, as part of the sweeping cultural changes of the 1960s, the Catholic laity responded with a combination of confusion and anger as the richly detailed surroundings of their local churches gave way to high modern iconoclasm. Stripping churches of their pre-Vatican II appointments and literally scrubbing their interior surfaces clean of applied color and decoration in fact became for architects the most expedient means of fulfilling the letter of post-conciliar law (figs. 36a and b). To the average layperson, however, the forced abandonment of architectural conventions maintained by Roman Catholicism for centuries was nothing less than traumatic.

That large numbers of Catholics in the United States continue in their disdain for the kinds of spaces modern architecture offers them for worship is attributable, I would suggest, to an admixture of deep-seated religious instincts and an appetite for material clutter acquired from the dominant market culture. Today, after all, the attitudes of American Catholics concerning their physical environments are shaped as much by Sabbath hours spent circuiting the local retail malls as by time spent in church. The former provide them some slick, prepackaged semblance of communal space, tradition, and seasonal ritual; the latter presumes to offer the real things. To their appraisal of sacred architecture Catholics also bring a wide range of ethnic predilections, habits of personal piety, and the impression of overwrought catalog merchandise that for years has set the unofficial standard for the liturgical decorum maintained in parishes across the country. Among conservative Catholics especially there endures as well an attachment to church buildings on the basilican model—hierarchically arranged, full of fancy stencilwork, stained glass and gilding, and capable of a kind of scenographic presentation of liturgical action. The problem with modernism as a liturgical style, at least at its most aloof and cerebral, is that it makes few concessions to such popular sentiments; neither does it accommodate very well the inherent messiness that Catholic sacramentality involves, its indulgence in layered sensuality and a range of human emotions not easily confinable to the tidy conceptual schemes of architects and liturgists.

Some Architectural Examples

Tempering modernism's inflexibility while maintaining an approach to design based on measure and restraint seems to have been the intention of Richard Podulka (North Park Studio, Berea, Ohio), project architect for the 1994 renovation of the Magnificat Chapel at Villa Maria, Pennsylvania (figs. 37–40; see color insert). The chapel, property of a local community of the Sisters of the Humility of Mary, suffered from midcentury modern décor that had grown

Fig. 36b—Catholic church interior after Vatican II renovations.

stale and unappealing. Of greater concern to the community, however, were deficiencies in the building's functional plan, whose fixed seating and detached sanctuary worked against liturgy that was inclusive of the entire assembly. In its revised form the chapel's main worship hall houses an ensemble of portable furnishings that may be freely arranged according to the community's changing needs. For worship, altar and ambo most often stand as foci on the hall's longitudinal axis and are bracketed by broad arcs of metal-frame chairs, the latter of which were selected for their graceful, curvilinear contours. Recurrent throughout the main hall and a newly created chapel of reservation, in fact, are fluid shapes that counter the severe angularity of the building's structural shell. The introduction during renovation of natural materials, colors, and textures likewise has softened the effect of the surrounding geometry and contributes to an atmosphere that is at once warm and serene.

Similar results have been achieved at Mount Irenaeus Chapel in Friendship, New York (figs. 41–43; see color insert), designed in 1989 by Pittsburgh-based KSBA Architects for a retreat center operated by St. Bonaventure University (Olean, New York). Situated in the wooded foothills of southwestern New York State, Mount Irenaeus consists of an unassuming timber-frame structure with plank siding and a foundation of native stone. Except for a cross at the peak of its west gable, the building bears no external sign of sacred function but seems nevertheless to fulfill its owners' wishes for a place marked by "beauty, integrity and simplicity."[2] The chapel's intimate liturgical setting, virtually square in plan, allows lay worshipers to gather at three sides of a centralized altar, the legs of which are fashioned from tree trunks taken from the site. Seating is provided by tiered benches finished in gingham pillow-cushions that give the chapel an informal, almost domestic quality and one of its few sources of decorative color. The chapel's unadorned walls are dominated by windows that, consistent with the Franciscan spirituality that informs this place, offer generous views of a surrounding landscape that is itself perceived as a sign of God's incarnate presence in the world.

Renovation in 1993 of a free-standing chapel at St. Matthew-in-the-Woods Parish in Summit Township, Pennsylvania (Crowner/King Architects, Erie, Pennsylvania; figs. 18–20; see page 51 and color insert), involved dramatic reconfiguration of the liturgical plan and elimination of structural elements that tended to compartmentalize the building's modest interior volume. Decades of eclecticism had left the sanctuary filled to capacity with a confusing array of nonliturgical objects, and the bulky furnishings of the nave made ritual movement cumbersome. The revised arrangement puts altar, ambo, and presider's chair on a low bema platform that extends from a side wall into the rectangular body of the church, where it is surrounded by compact groupings of movable chairs. A tabernacle stand occupies the center of what had been the chapel's shallow apse. Owing to local opinion, a rather overscaled crucifix was left attached to the apsidal wall behind the tabernacle, while the parish's remaining sculptural images were removed to a small narthex that now doubles as a shrine room. New slate flooring and a paint scheme favoring grays and black provide a neutral backdrop for blocky,

2. From the clients' programmatic statement, provided by KSBA Architects, Pittsburgh, Pennsylvania.

Fig. 19—St. Matthew-in-the-Woods Church, Summit Township, Pennsylvania. Interior after renovation.

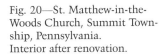

Fig. 20—St. Matthew-in-the-Woods Church, Summit Township, Pennsylvania. Interior after renovation.

Fig. 24—St. John the Baptist Church, Erie, Pennsylvania. Interior after renovation.

Fig. 25—St. John the Baptist Church, Erie, Pennsylvania. Interior detail.

Fig. 37—Magnificat Chapel, Villa Maria, Pennsylvania.
Worship room interior after 1994 renovation.

Fig. 39—Magnificat Chapel,
Villa Maria, Pennsylvania.
Detail with altar.

Fig. 38—Magnificat Chapel, Villa Maria, Pennsylvania.
Detail with ambo.

Fig. 40—Magnificat Chapel, Villa Maria, Pennsylvania.
Eucharistic reservation chapel.

Fig. 41—Mount Irenaeus Chapel, Friendship, New York (1989). Exterior.

Fig. 42—Mount Irenaeus Chapel, Friendship, New York. Interior.

Fig. 43—Mount Irenaeus Chapel, Friendship, New York. Interior.

Fig. 48—St. Joseph Cathedral, Wheeling, West Virginia (renovated 1996). Nave interior.

Fig. 49—St. Joseph Cathedral, Wheeling, West Virginia. Sanctuary detail.

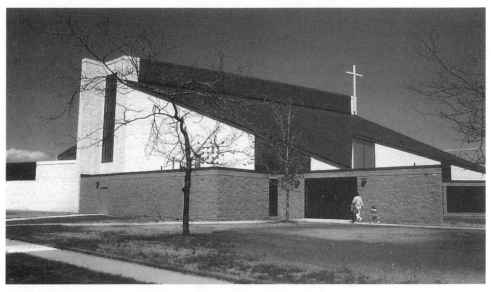

Fig. 44—St. Barnabas Church, Depew, New York (1993). Exterior.

wooden appointments and lend this once quaint and rustic chapel a crisper, more finished appearance.

Conclusions

Perhaps it is only in specialized and modestly scaled projects such as these that simplicity—"noble" or otherwise—has much chance today of being obtained. So contentious is the task of building for large, heterogeneous, and vastly opinionated parish communities that even the sincerest building committees can be tempted to ignore lofty episcopal pronouncements for the sake of collective sanity and practical survival. At St. Barnabas Parish in the suburban fringes of Buffalo, New York, for example, recent construction has resulted in a massive, accordion-shaped edifice (figs. 44 and 45) that competes for monument status with

Fig. 45—St. Barnabas Church, Depew, New York. Interior.

Fig. 46—Holy Redeemer Church, Warren, Pannsylvania (1994).

neighboring buildings along a busy, commercial strip. Barely was the paint on the church's interior walls dry before parishioners began filling the place with leafy plants and objects preserved from their former facility. At the new Holy Redeemer Church in Warren, Pennsylvania (figs. 46 and 47), formal simplicity

was compromised by imposition of a colossal, fiberglass corpus on the building's public façade and by interior spotlights, suspended near each window, that transform the church at night into something of a giant, stained-glass lantern. At the renovated (1996) St. Joseph Cathedral in Wheeling, West Virginia (figs. 48 and 49; see color insert), simplicity has been concealed beneath Aztec-inspired murals from the 1920s and hundreds of freshly painted ceiling coffers. And at St. Peter Cathedral in Erie, Pennsylvania (figs. 50 and 51; see page 106 for fig. 51), three layers of gilding, expanses of newly imported marble veneers, and furnishings of ponderous shapes and sizes together do the trick.

Fig. 47—Holy Redeemer Church, Warren, Pennsylvania. Exterior detail.

Whether these latter structures should be taken as authentic expressions of a hybrid culture that is as much American as it is Catholic is uncertain; they may simply reflect the influence of designers and vendors whose businesses stand to profit more from the expansion of building projects than from their containment. What one senses from the current state of Catholic architecture in the United States, however, is that parishes and professional designers alike could benefit from a wider view of the Church's own artistic heritage, which records more than the decorative excesses and triumphalism of recent centuries. It was from Catholicism, of course, that there long ago emerged Gregorian plainsong and the exquisite austerity of Romanesque building forms put to monastic purpose. The directness of the Church's salvation narrative, coupled

Fig. 50—St. Peter Cathedral, Erie, Pennsylvania (renovated 1993).

Fig. 51—St. Peter Cathedral, Erie, Pennsylvania. Interior detail with cathedra.

with a classical strain of religious expression, infected the verse of Dante, the paintings of Giotto, Fra Angelico, Raphael; Michelangelo's masterworks; the churches of Brunelleschi and Alberti, of Palladio. It was the catalyst behind the tightly bound Mass settings of Mozart, Haydn, and other members of the eighteenth-century Classical Viennese School of composition and can be spotted today in the poetry of Thomas Merton and in the moving, relationship-filled novels of Graham Greene, Flannery O'Connor, and Mary Gordon; in the sacred music of Krysztof Penderecki or Jean Longlais or Lucien Deiss; in churches by Germany's famous Böhm family. Indeed, examples abound in Catholic tradition of art that results from what is essentially a subtractive or poetic process, one that seeks to pare away from the central, declarative statement anything that might obfuscate meaning or appear overly self-referential. Thus, by establishing for its liturgical environment a standard of "noble simplicity," the Catholic Church has not invited contemporary artists and architects to operate in entirely new ways or with a façile and style-conscious "Less is More" sort of asceticism. In the end the issue for the Church has little to do with artistic style, anyway, or with trendy approaches to building and image-making. What matters most in our frenetic and solipsistic age is liturgy itself, which offers people reason to be connected to each other and to their God—even as elsewhere the experience of simple, human community appears in general decline. If, at the outset of the third millennium, liturgy for American Catholics is to remain an inescapably communal affair, if it is to be preserved from decaying into hollow, religious theater, it will require, by the Church's own admission, physical settings that serve honestly, without pretense or easy spectacle, and with forms whose very simplicity may indeed prove to be revelatory.

LIST OF ILLUSTRATIONS

1. Laurentian Library, Florence, Italy (1523–52). Michelangelo. *Ricetto* interior with staircase. Photo: DeTolnay, Charles, *Michelangelo: Painter, Sculptor, Architect*. Copyright © 1975, Princeton University Press. Reprinted by permission.

2. Laurentian Library, reading room interior. Gannon University Archives, Rev. Howard V. Niebling Collection.

3. Vietnam Veterans Memorial, Washington, D.C. (1982). Maya Ying Lin. Photo: Michael E. DeSanctis.

4. Vietnam Veterans Memorial, detail. Photo: Michael E. DeSanctis.

5. Early Christian House-Church at Capernaum (First–Fourth Century). Illustration: Michael E. DeSanctis after Corbo.

6. Early Christian House-Church at Dura-Europos, Syria (232–33). Illustration: Michael E. DeSanctis after Kraeling, Pohlmann.

7. Roman Basilica, Silchester, England (Second Century). Reconstruction. Illustration: Michael E. DeSanctis after Parrish.

8a. Basilican Church of San Clemente, Rome, Italy (Fourth Century, rebuilt, 1099–1108). Plan. Illustration: Michael E. DeSanctis after Fletcher.

8b. Basilican Church of San Clemente. Interior detail with *schola*. Photo: Gannon University Archives, Rev. Howard V. Niebling Collection.

9. Post-Vatican II Centralized Church. Our Lady of Grace Church, Greensburg, Pennsylvania (2000). Plan. Copyright © 1999, Prisco, Serena, Sturm Architects, Chicago, Illinois. Reproduced with permission.

10. Our Lady of Grace Church, Greensburg, Pennsylvania. Interior. Photo: Michael E. DeSanctis.

11. St. Mary Church, Meadville, Pennsylvania (constructed 1955; renovated 1994). Exterior. Photo: Michael E. DeSanctis.

12. St. Mary Church, Meadville, Pennsylvania. Interior before renovation. Photo: St. Mary Parish Collection.

13. St. Mary Church, Meadville, Pennsylvania. Interior after renovation. Photo: St. Mary Parish Collection.

14. St. Mary Church, Meadville, Pennsylvania. Nave interior from bema. Photo: Michael E. DeSanctis.

15. St. Mary Church, Meadville, Pennsylvania. Eucharistic reservation chapel. Photo: Michael E. DeSanctis.

16. St. Matthew-in-the-Woods Church, Summit Township, Pennsylvania (constructed 1936; renovated 1994). Exterior. Photo: Michael E. DeSanctis.

17. St. Matthew-in-the-Wood Church, Summit Township, Pennsylvania. Interior before renovation. Photo: Crowner/King Architects, Erie, Pennsylvania. Used with permission.

18. St. Matthew-in-the-Woods Church, Summit Township, Pennsylvania. Axonometric plan of renovation. Copyright © 1994, Crowner/King Architects, Erie, Pennsylvania. Reproduced with permission.

19. St. Matthew-in-the-Woods Church, Summit Township, Pennsylvania. Interior after renovation. Photo: Michael E. DeSanctis.

20. St. Matthew-in-the-Woods Church, Summit Township, Pennsylvania. Interior after renovation. Photo: Michael E. DeSanctis.

21. St. John the Baptist Church, Erie, Pennsylvania. Exterior. Photo: Michael E. DeSanctis.

22. St. John the Baptist Church, Erie, Pennsylvania. Interior ca. 1945. Photo: Erie County Historical Society, Inventory of Churches, City of Erie, Pennsylvania.

23. St. John the Baptist Church, Erie, Pennsylvania. Renovation plan. Copyright © 1993, Crowner/King Architects, Erie, Pennsylvania. Reproduced with permission.

24. St. John the Baptist Church, Erie, Pennsylvania. Interior after renovation. Photo: Michael E. DeSanctis.

25. St. John the Baptist Church, Erie, Pennsylvania. Interior detail. Photo: Michael E. DeSanctis.

26. Illustration accompanying the word "church" from *Catholic Picture Dictionary*. Copyright ©1948, Catholic Manufacturing Company. Used with permission.

27a and 27b. Images of church interior from Catholic grade school reader. Copyright © 1952, 1942, Ginn and Company. Used with permission of Scott Foresman.

28a and 28b. Images of church interior from Catholic grade school reader. Copyright © 1952, 1942, Ginn and Company. Used with permission of Scott Foresman.

29. Cover illustration from *Musica Sacra et Sacra Liturgia*. Copyright © 1958, National Catholic Welfare Conference. Used with permission of United States Catholic Conference.

30. Image of church façade from *St. Joseph Baltimore Catechism*. Copyright © 1962, Catholic Book Publishing Co., New York, N.Y. Used with permission.

31. Illustration from *We Go To Mass*. Copyright © 1987, Malhame and Company. Used with permission.

32. Promotional illustration for *Christ Our Life* series. Copyright © 1983, Loyola Press. Used with permission.

33. Illustration from *The Christian Community*, by Carl Pfeifer and Janaan Manternach. Copyright © 1977, Silver, Burdett and Ginn, Inc. Used with permission of Scott Foresman.

34. Illustration from *Jesus Teaches Us*, Copyright © 1990, St. Paul Books and Media. Used with permission of Gayle McNeil Bookmakers.

35. Child's drawing of a church.

36a. Traditional Catholic church interior before Vatican II. Photo: St. Mary Church, Erie, Pennsylvania. Parish Archives.

36b. Catholic church interior after Vatican II renovations. Photo: St. Mary Church, Erie, Pennsylvania. Parish Archives.

37. Magnificat Chapel, Villa Maria, Pennsylvania. Worship room interior after 1994 renovation. Richard Podulka architect, North Park Studio, Berea, Ohio. Photo: Copyright © 1994, Peter Renerts Studio, Cleveland, Ohio. Used with permission.

38. Magnificat Chapel, Villa Maria, Pennsylvania. Detail with ambo. Photo: Copyright © 1994, Peter Renerts Studio, Cleveland, Ohio. Used with permission.

39. Magnificat Chapel, Villa Maria, Pennsylvania. Detail with altar. Photo: Copyright © 1994, Peter Renerts Studio, Cleveland, Ohio. Used with permission.

40. Magnificat Chapel, Villa Maria, Pennsylvania. Eucharistic reservation chapel. Photo: Copyright © 1994, Peter Renerts Studio, Cleveland, Ohio. Used with permission.

41. Mount Irenaeus Chapel, Friendship, New York (1989). Exterior. KSBA Architects, Pittsburgh, Pennsylvania. Photo: KSBA Architects. Used with permission.

42. Mount Irenaeus Chapel, Friendship, New York. Interior. Photo: KSBA Architects. Used with permission.

43. Mount Irenaeus Chapel, Friendship, New York. Interior. Photo: KSBA Architects. Used with permission.

44. St. Barnabas Church, Depew, New York (1993). Exterior. Weborg/Rectenwald/Buehler Architects, Erie, Pennsylvania. Photo: Michael E. DeSanctis.

45. St. Barnabas Church, Depew, New York. Interior. Photo: Michael E. DeSanctis.

46. Holy Redeemer Church, Warren, Pennsylvania (1994). Strickland/Best Architects, Cranberry, Pennsylvania. Photo: Copyright © 1993, Lake Shore Visitor. Reproduced with permission.

47. Holy Redeemer Church, Warren, Pennsylvania. Exterior detail. Photo: Copyright © 1993, Lake Shore Visitor. Reproduced with permission.

48. St. Joseph Cathedral, Wheeling, West Virginia (renovated 1996). Nave interior. Celli/Flynn Architects, Pittsburgh, Pennsylvania. Photo: Copyright © 1996, Jim Schafer Location Photography. Reproduced with permission.

49. St. Joseph Cathedral, Wheeling, West Virginia. Sanctuary detail. Photo: Copyright © 1996, Jim Schafer Location Photography. Reproduced with permission.

50. St. Peter Cathedral, Erie, Pennsylvania (renovated 1993). Weibel, Rydzewski, Schuster Architects, Erie, Pennsylvania. Photo: Copyright © 1993, Lake Shore Visitor. Reproduced with permission.

51. St. Peter Cathedral, Erie, Pennsylvania. Interior detail with cathedra. Photo: Copyright © 1993, Lake Shore Visitor. Reproduced with permission.

INDEX

Iconoclasm
    Post-Vatican II architectural changes
        perceived as, 100
Immigrant Catholics
    in the U.S., generous giving habits of, 62
    sensibilities shaped by historical inherit-
        ance and new-found prosperity, 38
Incarnation
    mirrored in sacramental acts, 36
    sanctifying miracle of, 19
    offers us flesh-and-blood Messiah, 83
Informality
    condition of today's church-goers, 16–17,
        83
Intelligibility
    in liturgical expression, 38

Jacobs, Jane
    *The Death and Life of Great American
        Cities*, 2 n. 1
    and loss of place identity in the U.S., 81
Jaffe, Norman, Gates of the Grove Synagog,
    34
Jesus through the Centuries
    See Jaroslav Pelikan
John Paul II
    and use of modern-style crosier, 74
Johnson, Philip, 71
Jones, E. Fay, Thorncrown Chapel, 34

Kahn, Louis, 71
Kaza, Rev. Msgr. Charles, 52–55
Kline, Calvin, 83
KSBA Architects, Pittsburgh, Pennsylvania,
    102
Kunstler, James Howard, *The Geography of
    Nowhere*, 80–81

Laity
    exclusion from church design discussions
        before Vatican II, 8
    weary of liturgical changes, 4
Language, liturgical
    as cause of division in Church, 60–61
    and confusion over, 10
Lauren, Ralph
    and casual chic, 83
Laurentian Library, Florence
    as spatial journey, 26–27
Lavanoux, Maurice
    and criticism of mid-20th century liturgical
        art, 38
Lin, Maya Ying
    and design of Vietnam Veterans Memorial,
        27

Liturgy
    popularly exempted from analysis, 3
Longlais, Jean, 106

Magnificat Chapel, Villa Maria, Pennsylvania,
    101–102; *See also* color inserts, 3–5
Marx, Karl, 71
May, Rollo
    and human response to beauty, 24
McInerny, Ralph
    and *Catholic Dossier*, 15n.
McLuhan, Marshall, 71
Mediator Dei
    and liturgical participation of assembly,
        31, 91
Mediocrity
    weakens authority of the Church's
        message, 87
Merton, Thomas, 106
Michelangelo, Buonarotti
    and the Laurentian Library design, 26–27
    as creative innovator, 68
"Mod"
    as 1960s–70s popular fashion style, 72
Modern art, 65–75
Modern churches
    popular response to, 5, 69–70
Modernism
    late arrival to the Church, 99–100
    influence on post-Vatican II church design,
        17, 72
    as challenge to immutability of sacred art,
        99
    as threat to tradition, 67–68, 99
    as threat to community, 68–70
    as threat to sensual object, 70–73
    reappraisal of in church architecture, 18
Moratorium, on church architecture
    author's proposal for, 63
Moses
    model for pastors who renovate churches,
        41
Motu proprio
    on sacred liturgy of Paul VI, 41–42
    on sacred music of Pius X, 31
Mount Irenaeus Chapel, Friendship, New
    York, 102; *See also* color inserts, 6–7
Mozart, Wolfgang, 106
Mumford, Lewis, 1

NASA, 23
National Conference of Catholic Bishops
    and author's proposal for 63–64
Niebuhr, Reinhold, 2 n. 1